THE

DOA

DEAD ON ARRIVAL

Who Made It!

Are You Ready to Take
Your Last Breath?

DAVID MILES

WestBow
PRESS
A DIVISION OF THOMAS NELSON

WestBow Press books may be ordered through booksellers or by contacting:

WestBow Press
A Division of Thomas Nelson
1663 Liberty Drive
Bloomington, IN 47403
www.westbowpress.com
1-(866) 928-1240

ISBN: 978-1-4908-0469-9 (sc)
ISBN: 978-1-4908-0470-5 (hc)
ISBN: 978-1-4908-0471-2 (e)

Library of Congress Control Number: 2013914732

Printed in the United States of America.

WestBow Press rev. date: 08/16/2013

Dedication

To my wife and sons

Whom I love and admire so much and especially to my

mom and dad, who taught me something by example

rather than curriculum; which was the simple Biblical

concept of contentment.

And to all of my friends /acquaintances who claim

to like me, but probably just do it out of sympathy

Table of Contents

Authors Biography

Associates Degree, Concordia College, Milwaukee, WI.

Bachelor of Arts Degree, Concordia University River Forest, Ill.

Certified Financial Counselor, Crown Financial Ministries Ga.

Ordained Pastoral Ministries Fellowship Bible Ministries, Milwaukee, WI.

Certified small engine mechanic: Evinrude Motors, Arctic Cat co. Kawasaki Motors. USA

Certified Battery Technician: Batteries Plus LLC.

The D.O.A . . . Who Made It!

This is the true story of David Miles. His first–Life & Death experience, and "after life encounter with GOD. Yes God. He (I) did talk with God. And our conversation was VERY Real!

Its' Not just another action packed exciting book about someone who's seen a light at the end of a tunnel (usually a train coming). I'm just a plain old ordinary person, from the Milwaukee area, who grew up in the '50's and '60's. I went to college to be a Lutheran Pastor, and ended up selling motorcycles most of my life.

I do want to say, that after you see the "death" experiences that I have encountered, you will find this book very stirring, stimulating, introspective, and as to the reality of LIFE! *Here*, and *Here-After.* Are genuinely and as true as it gets.

Are You the kind of person that thinks "*God Deserves His Due's*? Do You really believe that you've got something to offer Him—That He Can and Should Accept?

Acknowledgment

First, I want to thank you, the readers that can make it

All the way through this book.

I especially thank all of the people who participated in

saving my life, through their care, consideration courageous

and determined help in keeping me alive; from the road to the

hospital & to all of the "care-takers" of my wellbeing.

But most of all; I have to thank the GOOD LORD, for:

believe it or not; putting me through this.

If you think that sounds crazy, just keep reading.

I might say "some things" about a motorcycle company
that's based here in Milwaukee, WI. But if it wasn't
for them and their predecessor Triumph (1902)

& Indian Cycles, (1901)

none of this would have happened, {I'm sure}. They did get the attention of the American/world public to recognize motorcycling as a very real valid fact of life

for so many people. So, I, "heartily," thank You

For making the lives of so many people, {bikers, dealers, employees, etc.} so enjoyable.

All Biblical references from (KJV) King James Version; unless noted

Great appreciation to my son Eric, and Shelby, and Dayton, who helped me edit this book

Some Names were changed to protect the innocent, and even the "not so innocent".

Preface

This book may not be as exciting as last night's game, or

the movie you saw on the weekend; but I assure you.

After you read it, You won't just go to sleep tonight and

forget what you read.

More than a quarter century ago, I "met my maker" and you know

what . . . It was very real. To the point that "life after death" is

<u>simply No Joke.</u>

"Science" Does Not "have all the answers," and I am about to

clearly prove that in these pages.

Once you've been dead, and come back to life the
"unbelievers" words are pure fictional <u>nonsense.</u>

This book gets pretty funny for guys and gals alike

Please: Enjoy the read.

<u>Ephesians 2:8 & 9</u>

For by Grace are you saved

through faith.

It is the Gift from God

Not of Works

Lest anyone should boast

"THE D.O.A . . . WHO MADE IT!"

**Living proof of what Will really Happen
"After" YOUR last breath!**

Introduction

HUMAN CANNONBALL? . . . Mythical Flying Super Hero? . . . Crazy Stuntman? . . . What is going on here? Those were some of the questions that must have been surely going through the minds of the many motorists now gridlocked, at a very large and busy highway intersection, at 6:02 in the afternoon, on a hot and sunny, summer Tuesday {July 1ˢᵗ.} just outside Milwaukee, WI.

Two weeks later:

Arms and legs, strapped down tight, to a bed railing. Regaining consciousness; I found myself staring at what I was sure were "prison walls." Right at that moment, I was so terrified for my safety and well-being. Feeling horrified; till suddenly, two young brightly dressed girls in red & white uniforms, jumped up and out of their chairs that were near the foot of my bed. Both desperately trying to settle me down from my convulsive acts of writhing with straps & hoses restricting me to a bed that I had no idea why I was in. I noticed that it was slightly canted up just enough so I could see just a little at the foot of the bed. But OH Oh! That's when, It Hit! The razor sharp **Pain,** all around my body and head. "What's Going On?" I cried out.

Struggling and thrashing all the more, in a desperate panic scream I pleaded; "Where am I, What's going on, what's happening to me? Please someone . . . *Let me Go!*" "Relax Mr. Miles, you're in St. Lou's hospital now; you were in a horrible accident, 2 weeks ago".

What! No! I wasn't in any accident; while gagging on my tongue and all of the debris in my throat. I am on my way home for tacos, before I have to go to a deacon/elder meeting, out in Muskego. I don't want to be late. Let Me Go—Now!"

NO . . . No, we can't let you go, you are hurt, way too bad. You are in St. Lou's hospital (The best *trauma* hospital in S.E. Wisconsin). {Great . . . just what I needed after that news, was a commercial, about a hospital.} "Please just let me go." The one girl then said "After that terrible crash, that you were just involved in; and you were actually **"killed dead"** {is there any other way to be" killed?}, you have to stay here and get healed." "I was WHAT? Killed to death," The other girl then quipped. "But see they were able to C.P.R. You & bring you back to life, and then they got you here to St. Lou's." WHAT . . . ? I thought; this just can't be. I know it's NOT a Joke; but what? I know that I'm on my way home to have supper, and go to a church leaders' meeting; that's all I know.

"WHAT! NO, "This just can't be true." I blurted out in a scream; the best I could with all the hoses shoved down both of my nostrils into my throat, and some big metal bracket wrapped around the upper part of my head, with bolts sticking into my skull, and my mouth was wired shut, so I could hardly talk, or move my mouth. I just left work. & I'm on my way home, on my new demo sport-touring cycle. By the way where is it?" I cried out, again with urgency. "Where is it? It's a brand new bike with only a hundred miles on it. Oh; Hank the owner really IS going to kill me, for sure when he finds that out." "Don't worry Mr. Miles, he and all your family know already." "What! How can any of this be?" I despondently, and very uncomfortably gruffed.

"We just can't let you go, Mr. Miles, please calm down and stop trying to pull all those tubes and hoses off. You've been hurt SO, SO Bad." "What? . . . This has to be some kind of horrific nightmare." I shrieked. But suddenly, at that point, I felt a tone of agreement with them, realizing that I did have all those hoses going into different orifice's, all over my head and arms, and even lower body. There was some sort of bracket around my jaw, and I was unable to move my mouth or jaw, but just my lips. They were all digging into my skin. And with that clear line of fluid stuck into my arm I really felt trapped. "My God!, what's going on here?" I quivered in fearful thought. When I finally settled a little, and quit trying to get myself out of bed, they then began to tell me the story of just what had taken place two, Yes! Exactly two weeks ago.

You see, I was a young married man, thirty five years old, with two very awesome, young sons, & I lived only about four miles away from my job, which was selling motorcycles, snowmobiles, Jet Ski's, atv's, boats and outboards. Our store was straight down the big main, "heavily traveled" highway. What I remember about that day was that it was a beautiful warm sunny Tuesday afternoon, a little after 6:00 pm (It stays very light at 6:00 pm, since it was July 1st).

On a very heavy controlled six lane major intersection known as U.S. Hwy 41, it's also called 27th St. in the city of Milwaukee, WI. I was going north toward home; and was sitting by myself at the front of the intersection in the left lane at a red light. There was a lot of cross traffic coming & going in front of me, on that big and busy cross way. Just so many people having busy lives of their own, rushing home or maybe to the store. Then seemingly out of nowhere . . . INSTANTLY! I was "**rear-ended**" by a car that was going "head on" into all of that cross traffics in the intersection with my motorcycle thrust into the front end of the car, leading the way, to even further destruction. Many of those cars would have been "doomed". It was going at almost fifty miles an hour, with no intention of even slowing a bit. The old four door sedan struck me at that speed & sent me flying upward through the air, three stories high, (if one is able to believe some thirty-three witnesses that were part of the two different police departments, report).

The End is Near!

At that busy intersection, my book-keeping gal, Kara, was next to me in the right lane. A younger man Al, who was one of my "set up" guys, was in the left hand turn median, heading west. But for a little short fat guy (not quite Danny Devi to, but close) to fly like that, must have been one "heckuva" a sight to see, But on the way back down it gets {better} yet. I then proceeded to make two beautiful reverse somersaults, (get jealous divers). Upon my landing, (it just so happened to be with my feet,) right on top of the car that had just hit me; I crushed in the roof just above the drivers head. But then my feet flew out forward, in front of me, as I was bouncing and I landed on the roof *again,* on my "touché". There's a lot more to that; later. (Ouch–to say the least). Now, after my "double bump" on the car that just {took me out} I then proceeded to fly almost a hundred feet to the other side of the three lane intersection, and amazingly enough, I did not hit any cross traffic (thank God no big high semis were going by just then). But come on! One of the two local police departments couldn't even give me a full one hundred feet, just 98.75'. So there goes my "frequent flier mileage". Oh well; things got a lot worse after that anyhow . . .

Chap. 1

Brief History

Let's see how this all started. Back in 1950, I was born in Milwaukee, Wisconsin, and my parents lived on the {Polish} south side. Back then most of the ethnic communities lived in almost distinct areas of the city. But we weren't even Polish. My mom (Joyce) is a full German lady, and my dad is a complete Irishman. So you figure that one out. Except the rents were a little less and for a newly married couple that was quite a necessity. My dad (Don) drove city bus and or street cars, and my mom worked for a big insurance company downtown.

where's E.E.O.B when you need 'em?
(Equal Employment Opportunity Bureau)

{Gals; you're gonna just love this part}. This big insurance company, no a "Huge" insurance Co. had a corporate policy that said "any females working for the company, "<u>COULD NOT</u> "be or get married; or else they would lose their job." (ain't that ever somtin?) So her job worked out all pretty Okay, for a while any way. Till she had to quit. ('dem's, "da rules)

Yup, When I was almost a whopping three years old and "rarin'" to go My folks & I, (of course, they did take me along) moved out to a peaceful little lake, just about 20 miles southwest of Milwaukee. I was all by myself, (ya ya, an only child—I know what you're

1

thinking) spoiled brat. Okay, if having my very own sandbox in the back-yard, makes me spoiled I'd guess you'd be right. I must say though, I grew up pretty quick, just because the only people that I had to communicate and do things with, were adults, and some pretty old folks at that. Then I started to think I was headed in that direction anyway. (aren't we all?) But shortly after the ice was off of the lake, I pretty much made my company with a nice large school; (of fish, that is). So I grew up in the country, all by myself, except for that "smattering" of adults that lived in the area around the lake. I did have my dog (Slippers). He was a little mean cuss, though, to everyone but me; so that worked well, especially if I knew that I might be headed for a "spanking"

I really did get a lot of my "life's value's" education right by our next door neighbors. It was a swimming beach, picnic field with an attached woods and a big tavern/dance hall up by the main road. Which by the way wasn't much of a main road, back then either.

But by the time I was 8 years old, I could tap an "old fashion" keg of beer, for one of the picnic groups,(in case you thought that I was real thirsty), and I could almost lift a full wooden case of beer & sometimes soda bottles by myself. We would have to deliver, to all of the different picnic gatherers that came to the park in the summer to enjoy swimming and volleyball or baseball at their different company picnic outings, that were so popular back (in the those day).

Okay, so I wasn't *quite* born at (in) the lake, but as much time as I spent in the water, everyone thought that I had gills. And I was blessed enough to be already living at this beautiful clean clear spring feed lake, which I said was only about 20 miles west of lake Michigan. By the way the "Indian" name for this, Lake Denoon, was Moonish-Napish {the Moon's Looking Glass}. Pretty, no? There was not so much as 1 boat on the lake with a motor on it, in 1952; but that changed soon. Sorry Sierra Club members, **it was all our fault!**

But telling you that I was born right where they made Pabst, Schlitz, Miller, & Blatz beer, you'd have to expect me and everyone

2

else in Milwaukee/Southeast Wisconsin to be" *gut German"* beer drinkers. After all, we had "gemutlichkeit" {warm friendliness}, as long as we had a beer in hand.

(All of you "suds sippers") I didn't say {suckers} will love this). Back, until the late sixties and early seventies, if you worked at one of the breweries in the Milwaukee area, you were allowed to drink beer on the job, right while you were working. Now you see why we had such high employment back then; and everyone really loved their jobs.

So this is where, my strange life story begins to get pretty darn weird. Are you ready for this? Okay, So Here we go. Again, now as a young boy of eight or nine, I would do all kinds of odd-jobs around the tavern, dance-hall, swimming beach & picnic areas. But this is where it gets really fun; you see, as a hard working lad I got paid really *really* well. Yup; (at least from an 8 year old's point of view). When I was done with a certain day's chores, or some tasks with the owner's teenage sons, who worked all around the grounds. They would pay me with ice-cream sundaes,(hot fudge and caramel) and hot-dog /hamburgers, and even my very own "protected right", to go into the "penny-ante" candy counter, and enjoy ALL that I wanted. NOW; what kid could ask for more than that, huh, really, the ultimate-no?

Something <u>stinky</u> is brewing downstairs

This now leads to why I have an absolute total "disgust" for beer of any type. Because one of my duties over at the resort, was to, each and every day, or so, especially after parties and weekends, I had to go down in the huge drive-in basement in the front warm smelly corner, I would go in and sit on an empty beer bottle case and empty the chicken-mesh wired cage called the "bottle shoots" that held all of the "reeky" stench spewing opened & mostly empty bottles of aging now raunchy beer,(which was stewing in the summer heat) and put them into the cases for return to the beer delivery trucks.

Just try to imagine yourself, warm, sticky sweat on your own body then, day after day, sit in the heat of the summer, with hundreds of bottles, that each had a teaspoon/tablespoon of now fermenting beer sitting in it, very repulsively gross smell, and then having to take each one and right the bottle and put it in the old beer case. Believe me . . . It Was Putrid! So now you know where I got my lack of attraction for beer products. And let's be real honest, isn't that worth a couple of handfuls (washed) of candy, and say, maybe a chocolate soda, or hot fudge sundae?

walk home, To school?

Okay, So I wasn't the skinniest kid in the two room school house that had all eight grades under that one roof, with two teachers. There was just two others in my grade, and we had about 16 students in first thru fourth grade down stairs. The fifth thru eighth (the *big kids*) were upstairs. Now you are not going to believe this (I'm almost willing to bet) but the two room school, was about ½–3/4 of a mile from our house, and YES I did have to walk it each and every school day. (yup, it was up hill both ways, even in the snow, when I had to walk it barefoot-ha ha). No! Really; the neighbor girl from the farm down the road and I walked the side of the road to and from, each and every day. After two years her younger brother would walk with us, too. We both started that in first grade.

We played hard and took total advantage of each and every recess that we got on those school day. (texted our friends, call home on our cell, played video games—I think Not), the school building didn't even have a telephone. We played all sorts of activities, (mostly our own home-made games & rules. But wow, did we have fun, and I burned a lot of calories, & didn't even know that I was doing myself so much good.

For the next five grades, I was a student in that two room brick building, now looking back it almost seems like a type of home-schooling! We weren't crowded and we sure did get a lot of the teacher's attention. We said the *pledge of allegiance* every morning (hand on heart and "in God we trust"), then sang some, mostly patriotic songs. We even had a small stage in the back of the upstairs classroom and we would put on Christmas programs and the like.

Yardstick Justice?

Traveling teachers came in once or twice a week to teach us art and music. Maybe that was done for our protection (you'll see) and safety. Our "principal" Mrs. Ellertson was a very big stern senior woman. She had little patience in her character, for ANY misbehavior. When she gave out reprimands, they usually included some form of physical punishment with them.

My best friend Jerry, once jumped down the long set of stairs going out to recess. Mrs. Ellertson, saw this from the top of the stairs, and called him back up. As he very slowly-meekly wormed his way back up to the landing, she scolded him something fierce, and then broke a solid oak yard-stick in three places, over his head and told him how to behave. Yes that was severe, but a strong learning lesson for him, and all of us that saw it take place.

Da Vinci or Rembrandt?

Just as an *aside,* our art teacher, who was a younger fella, maybe in his twenties, would read some of the Greek mythological stories (like Iliad and the Odyssey) while reading, he would draw some scenes on the black board (yup, it really was black with white chalk). He would bring in his own colored chalk, and draw out on the board a big scene from part of what he read. I had a great view, because I was assigned the front seat in the front row, in the middle of the classroom). Who Me? {I was an angel . . . Not} normally, he would give each of us a big sheet of blank drawing paper and have us draw & color our version of the scenes that he had put on the board. That was the occasion of my first "real" academic scare. One of those "art class" day I drew out with a pencil a really cool scene. But when I got down near the edge of the bottom left-hand corner of the page, I suddenly realized that I didn't leave quite enough room for the officers' tent. This was a big "no-no" because on his insistence, we always had to border the paper with the classic Greek interlocking square design border. I thought NOW, WHAT?! I feared that I would have to start all over again, and I had even started coloring it, and it was almost lunch time! (OK, as usual, food on the brain)

In the "panic" mode, I was in, this gutsy (stupid?) fifth grader had the audacity to, actually erased part of the border and made the officers tent override the border! I sat there for a while before I was supposed to turn in the colored drawing. Boy, was I unsure of what to do now? Did I dare, Run down the stairs like I was sick and had to go to the bath room, or what? The art teacher came up from behind and startled me and looked down at the drawing that I knew was "marred". He then looked at me, and back at the picture. I thought I was "dead meat." To my surprise, and amazement. He picked it up and studied it more and as I was about to try to crawl out of the class-room for having pulled such a stunt. He calls out to the class to give their attention to my 2' X 3' art piece. (I really thought that I was going to get in big trouble). But the shocker was that he said that this was the best picture he had ever seen a fifth grader draw, because I had given it a "three-dimensional" look and that kind of "creativity" was what he was looking for. (go figure!)

Funniest thing though, ever since that episode, I began to love to draw, all sorts of things. He quite clearly gave me the motivation I needed to be a little daring in future attempts. Parents you might want to take note. (So then, now we know, it wasn't just because I was a lefty, but real encouragement). Another lesson I learned, for life.

"Cold Hard Criminal"

Before I had even gotten into first grade though, I became a "baaad "boy. As hopefully you'll see that, it didn't last long. A couple of miles from our house was a little itty bitty corner store at a somewhat busier intersection (busy out there was three cars an hour maybe. whew-hew) After church one Sunday, my mom and I would often go to the cute little country store to get some ham and rolls for lunch. While my mom was picking the cuts of ham, I spotted a little carousel, near a post, and while no-one was looking I picked up this "really cool", ball point pen. I examined it and clicked it a few times, and nonchalantly slid it into the pocket of my jacket. (Grand Theft Auto! Yikes). Well, when we got home and had our Sunday lunch, I was sitting in the kitchen and I pulled the pen out of my now pants pocket and started clicking it. After just a couple of minutes, my mom asked "Where did you get that pen?" Shrugging shoulders & mumbling gibberish, was all she got from me. She asked again! "Where did you get that pen from?" I softly replied. "The store" Knowing better," Did you have the money?" "And what store?" came right back at me. "The grocery store." I faintly said. "YOU STOLE THAT PEN!" She barked back at me, while she grasped me by the collar, and grabbing the pen away simultaneously.

"Put your coat on", she and I each did, and by my collar, she escorted me out like a ravenous animal. My mom always drives slowly, always, but not then; I'd swear she had it to the floor when we took off. It seemed like an "eternal instant", and we were back at that grocery store. We got out (she dragged me) and stormed up the few stairs, and went in. There was a loud horrible rattling noise that I could hear, just over the deep pounding of my heart, it was my knees banging together. Was I Scared!

We got to the counter and my mother held out the pen to the nice little old man who was a "live-in" owner, then she jammed it into my little clinched hand and said "Now give it back to the owner and apologize while you tell him what you did.

I was five and a half, and I was sure that I would never live to see my sixth birthday. I held my head down and mumbled again (I was getting good at the mumbling part). My mother put her hand under my chin, & yanked it up and said "look at him when you talk". So as I handed it back to him, I said "I'm Sorry" and he accepted the pen, without saying much. That was the first and last thing that I ever stole. And boy did it teach me another life lesson.

Two separate school districts merged, (maybe one just couldn't handle me?) so my seventh & eighth grade were spent in a k–8 school a little farther away. Yes right by the cute little store, I had robbed years earlier. I think my picture was still on the door? (well Maybe Not)

It's now my seventh grade and we were sitting in social studies class and the announcement came over the loudspeaker that the President of the United States had just been shot! We all panicked, and had no idea what to make of it. We had later heard that it had happened down in Texas. The president had died. That was one "eerie feeling" and as seventh graders we thought that the end was near, and we were all doomed, to having to become Communists.

Luv at first *row*?

On the brighter side of things; Back home again, a family friend named Hank, gave me a smaller 10' all wooden fishing boat to use out on the lake, I will say more about him later. That heavy wooden, little boat floated well, but was it a "bugger" to row. That beautiful 185 acre lake, got navigated by me a lot. Then for a young boy of maybe 12, I had biceps like a gymnast, (well, I wanted to believe it) Being an only child, and my dog didn't talk much (just bite people) I didn't get any sex education of any sort. But one day, I was rowing my little wooden "anchor-heavy" boat on another part of the lake when I saw this teen age girl swimming in front of her pier. Yes! It must have been when puberty hit. I didn't have a name for it, but I had a crush going, so hard on her, and my now big (to me at least) biceps, might really impress her; (ya think?) They didn't help . . . darn.

Another very interesting but deeply serious thing for a young boy to see and partake in, was when a swimmer in the big resort next door, would (for whatever reason) go missing. When a friend or family member would come up to one of the workers, or the life guard out in the boat, and tell us of the absence of one of their members. Many of us would dive down, (near the huge raft that was out from the clothes changing building on the beach) and search for the missing person. The extended swimming beach was over 200 feet long and almost pure sand. We would make everybody get out of the water, so it could clear, so we could maybe see the body.

Then the sand would continue way out in the now clear water) for almost another hundred feet; making this the most beautiful swimming beach and lake to be found in the area. The water was clean and clear, because it is spring fed. But after hours and hours of playing in the water, many people would walk to as deep as they could, in the lake, especially if they weren't swimmers themselves. Out another 45' was a huge 12 oil drum (barrel) raft and many of us would go diving around it; invariably someone would find the drowned swimmer, and usually before the rescue squad would even get there.

Most often the victim was a seemingly healthy male in his 20's, less often, (thankfully) it was a child. Those kind of drowning's occurred about once a year. The folks that were with the drowned person, almost always told us that they had been drinking "a lot." I saw C.P.R. several times. Once it even actually worked. Those were some real sad experience, but you know what. It taught me, back then, the possible "brevity" of life. My dad, also was a certified water patrolman on the lake, so we got called for incidents all around the lake cottages and houses.

Chap. 2

So Just Who is this guy?

For a family, we had it pretty darn well, even though we were almost as poor as "church mice". My mother should be taking care of our nation's finances, because she was so frugal and efficient, austerity wouldn't even come close as a definition. She grew up in the Great Depression, and she could stretch a dollar, but usually all we had was a couple of quarters so . . . you would be astounded. The presidents would cry, when they got squeezed so hard, and I think I saw a "buffalo nickel" poop once, when she had to put it out extra, for a purchase.

She had a system, (where she got it, I don't know) but she had a group of plain white small envelopes up in her dresser drawer, each one had a couple of dollars in them and something written on the outside of each, like food, insurance, heat, and she even had one for vacation. No credit cards, no loans, no ATM's, just very small amounts of cash, to pay the bills. Vacation! Yes, she even saved up for that.

And believe it or not we got to go all over America on vacation for about two weeks every year. We saw the Seattle World's Fair, Disney Land, (Disney World wasn't there yet) Washington, D.C. Williams burg, Va. Miami and Key West, Florida, New Orleans, Texas. We would go all over. The neatest thing was our family friend Hank, who would always offer his big late model "Buick and split the gas & motel bills with our family.

One time, when I was still very young (three or four), we took a vacation down to Mexico. I wore a pair of bright plaid shorts that were of mom's choosing, not mine, (common—I was four) and we stopped in a town to see a parade that they were having. (We liked parades). We parked and got out and stood in the crowd to see the floats and bands, and guess what; I couldn't see a thing. So Hank put me up on his shoulders, at first this was really nice. Then **ALL Of A Su**dden . . . I start squirming screeching and jumping around all over Hanks shoulders and his head and screaming out "OUCH *OUCH*!" Nobody knew what was wrong, but I sure made a commotion! So Hank lifted me off his shoulders, and I started to run in big circles, like a chicken with its head cut off. "What's the matter David?" my parents pleaded. Then I reached in my left pocket with another scream and pulled out a still burning cigarette butt, that someone ahead or alongside of us, must have flicked. It had landed right into my pocket, and started burning me. That put a big crimp into my parade viewing joy.

There, Is, Was, and I'm sure, never will, be, a more accurate navigator than my mom, either. She's really loaded with talent, isn't she. Every road, town and visitor sight, were calculated and calibrated to precision; for us to arrive there, where & when, and even if we would have enough gas to get there. You'd think that she was a human GPS, Really she was that good at it.

One, just One, and, only One, yes ONE, thing, that's all my dad was required to do on every vacation; (Hank always drove), and that was when we got to a motel, each time we would pull up to usually, a "mom & pop" 8-10 room motel. He was required (by mom) to go in and ask "how much would a room be for one night with 2 double beds?" He then went to the room (after he found out the rate usually about $6.00) and check the room "thoroughly" for the "dreaded" bed bugs, which my mother was deeply afraid of sharing the room with. So every time he would go in, and after a few minutes (we thought-inspecting) later came back out and let us know he didn't see or find, any bed bugs.

An interesting anecdote, is that years and years later, while sitting around the kitchen table, usually with my dad and our friend Hank; maybe playing "penny-ante" poker. My mom quipped how my dad NEVER found so much as one bed bug. Then the big confession came out. My dad conceded that "I couldn't tell you what a bed bug looks like, but I always knew the toilet flushed." There was a knife cutting glare, which my dad would have choked on, from mom, had we all not been laughing so hard!

Aye Aye Colonel

Do you remember "RADAR" from the TV show "MASH?" Well that was my dad too, in real life, during W.W.II. in Germany, not Korea. When his colonel would need or want something my dad would "attain it." for him. He got to Germany just as the war was ending, and there was plenty of "booty/plunder" for the "Upper ranks." My dad was sent out on a reconnaissance missions, to acquire it for the "brass." He had many funny and interesting stories war stories to relate to us. But, when he would be driving along, occasionally there was gun fire, sometimes aimed at him, from German "snipers" that didn't know the war was now over. So he would occasionally go on "midnight" requisitions.

As was discussed on vacation; we always got a room with 2 double beds (this was before king & queens were in). And guess how this worked. My mom and dad shared one bed, and Hank, our family friend, who most often came with us on those vacations, shared the other one, with me; well sort of. Hank had always been single. HE slept on a bit of a cot or just a hammock in the Navy, and I always slept in my own kids bed, and as a young boy from three years old till marriage, I never had any companionship; in bed.

This poor guy would get beaten up by me all night long. No, not with my big biceps-ha ha, but just by my "little kid" thrashing arms and legs. Often times, instead of waking anyone up, he would just get up and go sit on the chair out in front of the room, or somewhere close by. The problem was, Hank knew he would suffer later, because he would have to drive anywhere from 500–800 miles the next day. Looking back, I don't know how he did it.

Hank would often buy me something special on our trips, as a good reminder and souvenir. These gifts weren't big or expensive, but we seemed to some-how always get everything packed into the trunk of a pretty new Buick, and everyone sat in front, but me, so I had the whole back seat to myself. That wasn't really a very good idea. (Okay I'm spoiled-now keep reading)

Being alone in such a roomy back luxurious seat, it became real evident that it was a pretty bad thing to do (leave me in the car alone), once, when I was really little. While riding with Hank and my parents, at about age four or five, I discovered a cigarette lighter, mounted in the middle of the front and backseats, for some reason I was told to stay in the car while all of the others got out.

At times, it seemed like they were gone forever. So I became fascinated with this funny plug button that one could push in and it would heat up. I quickly found out that pushing it in, I could get it really hot, then I would push it in again and it would get really red some more. Eventually, I got the bright idea to push it against the back of the front seat, the vinyl would melt into the same shape as that lighter tip. I made a really cool pattern over the two week time, (I thought) and I was quite proud of it, (hey I was four) but, Yes I did keep it to myself! Alas one day many weeks after we got home, I was "severely" confronted with the fact that I was the only one ever in that back seat, and "just look what you have done!" Well, let me quickly say that . . . "lick-ins" were still approved and even legal back then, and did I, painfully learn another great big lesson OUCH! And worst yet my faithful companion dog, wasn't anywhere around for protection. This time.

Chap. 3

One Great Friend—Hank

I now have to tell you more about, our close family friend, Hank. He was really a great guy, who owned a busy truck stop/gas station, which from Muskego was back near the city of Milwaukee. Hank was in his mid-twenties, a veteran of WWII. He was involved in the landing of Iwo-Jima, as a U.S. Navy, Seabee. Actually {construction battalion} C.B. He was one of the soldiers who drove a bulldozer off a landing craft right into the ocean and up on to the beach. He heard the enemy bullets "zing" as they careened off the steel grid that protected the welded top, front & sides of the dozer.

Hank was a very wonderful and giving person, to my parents and I. Remember the little wooden boat? Because we were the only people he knew that weren't always trying to "get something for nothing", out of him And he also enjoyed the time he could spend out at the lake with my folks and I who became a kind of "surrogate" son he never had, on his own. He knew me since I was two years old. In my case, I never imagined life without him in it, or he without me. Hank's gas-station/truck-stop business was very successful, probably because after the war the roads were still just two lanes because, expressways weren't up and going yet, at least around us, his little corner gas station out in the country, back then. It was a good location because Hank did a huge amount of diesel truck business for the Cities Service Oil company (we now know it as Citgo).

As far back as I can remember, he would take me for rides usually he took me to his truck-stop or his parent's tavern and dinette; where we ate really *really* well. (It kept helping my figure) There was a pool table right in the middle of the bar-room. It was here that I learned how to shoot "8 ball" and I sure had a lot of fun doing that. (Especially, when I didn't have to put in the quarters. Is this how I learned to be frugal? Okay; so maybe I am a bit of a "cheapskate"

Hank had several nephews, who I eventually got to "hang out" with a lot. I saw the nephews at both the station and the bar. And we really hit it off well, for many years. They even showed me a lot of interesting things that an "only kid" might not learn on his own. These were "important things" like pounding a water pipe into the ground, and then dropping a fused lit "cherry-bomb" down into it, then (quickly) put a (pre-aluminum) soda can on the opening of the pipe. Boy, would that can go high up into the sky. It was really cool fun. (careful-now kids!)

Hank was a product of the prewar depression; and was the oldest of four children. He had three brothers and a sister. Wanting to go to school, was hard because, being the eldest boy, he had to stay back a lot and help do the farm chores, and raise his siblings. Prior to the war though, he did manage to get through the first grade of high school.

When he got back out of the Navy, with his C.B. experience he quickly got a job as a mechanic at a service garage, where he saved up every penny he had and got his own shop. It grew as he got busier, then he could afford to buy a gas/service station on the big main road going across country. This is where my parents got to know him, while my mom waitressed in a supper club across the street.

He built a big showroom building (all windows in front) just down on the end of the property but still on the main highway. He did this for a then small company called *Carver Boats*. Though small they made really high quality wooden boats, and started producing them right in the back of that building he leased to them.

Yes; they made great boats, and we lived on a nice lake, so guess what? Yup. He brought out a brand new gorgeous hand laminated all wood, Carver with a "whopping" huge 35 hp. Evinrude outboard motor, (this is about 1955 remember) It became the first boat with a motor on Moonish Napish, remember the Indian name for Lake Denoon, where we lived. Here, even, Hank and our whole family got to learn how to water ski. This little kid of about five or six, was given his very own, really short and stubby little pair of water skis. Hank truly, was a great friend to all of us. Small wonder I wasn't a bit spoiled *Spoiled* with a great friend like Hank.

Who says *"Spoiled"*

Getting back to my growing up, (which my wife is still waiting for.) Despite all the adventure I had with Hank, once–yes and only once, while growing up, did I ever get the opportunity to so much as sit on or take a short ride on a motorcycle, and it wasn't even on a public highway, just the long paved circular drive around the bathing resort and field next door. I had been on farm tractors and rode all over the grounds with a real cool 51 Ford pickup truck that even had a dump bed on it; really a pickup with a hydraulic dump bed, pretty cool, heh? And by now I had gotten to ride and drive snowmobiles, as well. (there were no atv's yet).

Hank, (the entrepreneur) decided to buy some; at the time, still a new idea, they were called snowmobiles. He didn't buy them to use, (right) but to resell (ha-ha). But most certainly they needed to be demonstrated. Of course, you know we had to "demo" them for customers, and in a little while, they were brought out to the lake country, where my folks lived that had lots of fields, and snowmobile trails all around our neighborhood, and they would go on for many miles.

So, I did get an opportunity to do a lot of snowmobile driving, and let me tell you folks that have never ridden. IT is a GREAT feeling! You don't even feel the cold when you're busy concentrating on the next bush or tree ahead of you (adrenalin pumping).

Let me say, that when I finally got on the back of a motorcycle (a young fella, who was a friend of a worker there for the summer) did I ever fall in LOVE with IT! I quickly said to myself "This IS What Really Makes Life Fun". Oh Yah . . . It Does!

But, now I learned the meaning of patience. (All these lessons were hard, for an adolescent, an only child living out in the country on a swimming/fishing lake). Every morning I was the first student picked up and then of course the last student dropped off of the school bus every afternoon.

This ride took over an hour to, and then from school. I just sat there just looking out the window waiting to arrive. Man that was hard. And that (twice a day) journey of over a full hour each way, sure taught me to appreciate when I did have something else that I could be doing. The worst part was that we went right by the school again two Different times on the route going around the different inland lakes that were in our area.

Looking back, it seems quite clear to me, that my experiences and character made me a person that savored action and participation. See, I don't know if it's my character, being an only child, or living out in the country, or what. But I personally think that just sitting on a bleacher, or in a stadium seat, watching a whole bunch of other people play, and then some of them to get paid for playing, is just a waste of time. When I am able I want to play, myself, rather than just watching somebody else have all the fun, and excitement. Maybe I was just a "biker", waiting to ride?

"Deadly Ping Pong"

While I was in the eighth grade The Vietnam war action was going on pretty strong, in 1964, while I was in the eighth grade. My mom & dad were very concerned about my being drafted in the "Ping-Pong" lottery program that the military was getting ready to implement. My mother, worked for a doctor whose opinion she deeply respected. She asked him for advice and suggestions about how to keep me out of this clearly "misguided" war. My parents were open to include even the idea of moving to Canada enabling me to escape the draft. (Hey—I was an "only" child)

As the war continued on longer and longer. More and more disturbing and disgusting truths began to surface like so many politicians having rice field investments over there that we were trying to protect; sure turned a lot of people off in the thought of "defending our country." Oh! All those poor soldiers over there getting killed; Why?

Well, this doctor told my mom to put me in some type of religious school, to obtain a religious degree or receive ordination; so that if I get out and get drafted, I would be one of the last ones sent to the front lines. Deciding to take his advice, my parents approached me and told me that they would send me to a Lutheran High School, either a Wisconsin or Missouri Synod, and there were two different ones in South-east Wisconsin, and I could pick which one I preferred. They even told me that they would pay for my tuition and board, I just had to pick the one I wanted to attend.

For the big "spiritual" decision I was about to make, I should pray, pondered and meditate all the differences over which one I wanted to go to, but I quickly asked them . . . (Please remember I was living at the beautiful sandy lake) "which one has a swimming pool"? (Pretty warm, and deep huh?)—Not the pool, but my religious and spiritual consideration. The school out in Watertown was a very conservative synod, and the other was just a little more "liberal." It was in the near west side of Milwaukee. The difference to me at that time in my life was the name of the state each put in from of their synod.

As I look back, this part of my life now makes me feel like I must have really "missed out." In other words, I was losing out on a lot in life, after all, it was the '60's and I was a health young man just waiting for life to come at me with all it had, yet, I am now enrolled and about to enter a very religious all "boys only high-school, and junior college, (1964—youngsters, go read some American history, if you don't understand what I'm talking about) life was just opening up for the youth of this country/world, to "live free". (Whew-hew!)

So, Concordia (boys only) High School and Jr. College here I come; girls or NO girls. (that's life . . . I guess)

You want to look, "really stupid"?

Was I now, "Spiritual" or just plain stupid, I can't say; but one beautiful Sunday morning in the middle of the summer, before I started ministerial school, our little conservative Synod Lutheran church, about 15 miles from our lake home, had its annual church picnic, but we also held our church service outside in a beautiful and serene shaded grove behind the church, where we all sat on folding metal chairs, for the day. There was a grassy aisle in the middle, and a movable church lectern that was up the front in the center.

For the life of me, I have no idea why I chose this one Sunday, but I sat all by myself in the far right corner of the front row of chairs, while my mom sat farther back with most of the other adults. So the service proceeded like a typical Lutheran service, and we sang several nice old hymns. Then the reading of the Gospels and Epistles, and then the pastor (whom I did laud and respect immensely) must have motioned to everyone in the congregation to sit down. Then he walked over to the little temporary podium and told us where the two portions of scripture would be coming from and he began to read them aloud. When he had finished, he began to give his "homily"-sermon, and I literally just stood there intently listening and mesmerized by his interpretation, yet I stood there like a statue (all by myself) for most of the whole 20-25 minute sermon. BOY! What an Idiot! I couldn't believe what I had just done. I was so humiliated when I sat down, and of course by myself, way up to the front. (Brain fart?) That probably was one of the most embarrassing moment of my life-(so far). I must confess, that I don't remember for sure, but I could almost "swear" that he was preaching on the story of Lazarus, who was Jesus good friend from Bethany. Maybe we'll find out; later.

Please, know that my intentions were not to go out and experience a "loose-life" of sex-drugs and rock & roll". But hey come on, it was the mid–sixties and I was a 14 year old. And just like any other "red-blooded" American boy, I had lots of hormones running around, "looking for luv." But there we were, in our *all boys* ministerial high-school & Jr. College, set to learn about God; (from the Missouri Synod's, rather conservative, point of view).

Wild S<u>e</u>xties?

The move to a multi-grade dormitory of 2 floors full of teen-age boys who really didn't want to be there, was as captivating as you could imagine, "Hazing" was the norm. Things like the first day before, class (a Sunday) there was an "official-looking" announcement to be at the swimming pool at 6:30 for a required "underwater basket weaving classes" This class was for "Sexties" only. What you say? No—it is Latin, for the number **six**, this was how many grades we had at that Jr. College/ High-school. The first Sunday we were all dropped off to start school the next day. School always had a lot of "newbies". So, we were all standing in a line outside of the pool, in our swimming suits, be it cold or warm out, we just stood there. After about twenty minutes and many older students walked by laughing profusely, we all just slunk away back to the dorm. But then the classes that the school did make us take were stupefying. Sure, there was the normal classes like English, World History, Social Studies, then Music, German & Latin; we had, no shop or tech instruction of any sort, this was to be our "labor in life".

We had, just really hard languages, with tons of memorization and grammatical rules. And guess what! The "professors: were pretty much like you'd suspect. They weren't passive or kind to us either in class or with their loads of home-work, for each class . . . We had to learn about every 14th, 15th 16th & 17th century composer. The classical Deutsche (Martin Luther German), Algebra, Social Studies. Plus every day we had chapel and Gym. It seemed like they had us write a report on something almost every day. But the studying and memorization never slacked off. Have you, ever had to do a report on how to do a report? (Yuk) And they never graded on a curve. Ouch!

I would not have admitted it then, but now I'll tell you that I really did learn a lot. Besides the complete biography of Mozart, Chopin, Brahms, Bach and all of their personal lives; we had a really cool Social Studies professor. He was pretty young (early 30's) but did he explain some great insight to all of his students. Simple things like "Why surge, after something that's falling and maybe hurt yourself, or someone else? It's only going to fall so far, the floor or ground" Use your head and your mind not your emotions! "Think through the logic of something, not just the superficial facade that most things offer." Sitting at a stop light next to someone you've never met; revving the heck out of your muscle car engine. Then taking off as fast as you can; tearing up your tires, sucking gas like a fish, just to prove *"a point"* to someone, you'll never even see again. Why-Ego. (Ewe) He was right. **"Just use your head."**

Talk about "one of those times," in my second year (sophomore-quinty) of high school, I was living on the second floor of a very long & large three story dormitory for the younger grades; and it was also the time of the mid-late sixties, when the national race relations were at their precipice of turmoil.

In Milwaukee, we were loudly denounced and reprimanded by a Caucasian Catholic Priest, named Father James Groppi; who led many rally's & "sit ins," all over the city of Milwaukee.

One late spring day, there was a march, going right past our dormitory, and of course a group of the sophomores had to show off and pitching pennies at the younger crowd. (mostly girls). We (almost) had our own "race riot" take place right on campus. Thankfully they decided to just keep moving along. (that was close)

"I Came, I Saw, I Conquered," but Not in Latin

Another challenge in going to that school, was, Latin. Our professor walked in the very first day of class loaded with brand new sexties, (that's all he'd call us, he wasn't loaded the room was) and started our brand new foreign language, by saying, "Look, Sexties, there is Nobody, except a few Catholic priests and pharmacists, that know anything about this "dead" language of Latin. But because *Jerome* wrote the *Vulgate* from Hebrew & Greek into Latin, the "church" believes that you should learn it too. So sit down, shut-up and open your books, and you better start learning NOW! It was my very first class, every morning, at that school at the start of the day. That sure gave us some enthusiasm-not!

That was our motivational speech to get us ready to really want to learn Latin. I did remember one thing, (and that's about it) from those 4 years of Latin, here it is. "Vini Vidi Vici" Julius Caesar's quote in 47 B.C., (yes that was before I was born-really) that says: "I came. I saw . . . I conquered". Then we were told years later, that, even that quote may not have been genuine at all, of Julius Caesar. But just, that, Shakespeare said it was so. I sure couldn't get to excited to learn Latin, but then came German, the old classical German. They use the same alphabet as English, and so many of our English words come from German. Now I wouldn't have admitted that either, but now I'll tell you that I really did learn a lot; besides the complete story of composers personal lives. We had a really cool history prof, and he really could bring out the facts of all these empires and people that attracted my attention; which may have been why I majored in history in college.

Shortest What?

Our, Religion professor, in actuality was the high-school's principal as well. He was old, and seemed really mean and tough, but a lot of it might have just been his "German" character. He did present us with some very interesting spiritual concepts, and principles that I will never forget. (Neither will you, when you get farther along.) Very sternly he commandingly asked all of us Sexties a question that he felt we should all know. The (20 some, students in that class). Because we all had come from "good" Lutheran, somewhat religious backgrounds, and attended our confirmation classes and also supposing that we all knew at least some of the Lutheran Catechism; plus things like the Nicene Creed. He felt we would all jump at the opportunity to answer his question, which was: "What's the SHORTEST verse in the Bible?" Guess what, not a student's hand went up, and he was "getting really miffed" at us. Try to imagine that scene; I'm not certain that there was steam coming from his nostrils, but there just may as well have been. **"It's in the Gospel of John, chapter, 11 verse 35.** Does anyone know where that is, and maybe know what it says?" "It's what I'm about to do, right now." he murmured. It says . . . "*Jesus wept*." "Boy's *Boy's*, what is wrong with all of you? How are you going to become church leaders someday, and you don't even know something this simple?" He bowed his head, as he pulled his glasses off and put his hands on his face covering his eyes, and stood there and just shook it in dismay.

There were four years of that, kind of pressure, and {believe it or not} we did truly get some intense learning. But when I was able to go to Germany some years later. I hardly knew a thing that anyone said; and they could barely understand a thing I said to them. The old classical/biblical German was very different from the modern German language spoken in the 20th century. Just like all of us walking around saying thee, thy, thou, and thus; from the King James English.

Coming back to school on our second year (Quinties), we found out that one of our classmates had died over the summer. He had been held back a couple of times, in his old school in Illinois. He had just turned 16 years old in the middle of summer, and of course started driving. Well he hit an electric pole in the dark one night and got out to "check things out" and stepped on the electric wire from the pole he just knocked over, and it killed him instantly. (another reminder)

As surprising as this might sound, when I went through school, typewriters were becoming an important part of life. Electric typewriters weren't quite out yet. The radically new IBM "floating" ball. All we did have were some of the old Royal mechanical typewriters that we had to learn how to type on, and you really had to "plunk" down hard on those keys to make it through the ribbon to the paper. (Carpel-tunnel anyone)Yes I was a lefty, and all I could remember as a little child, from people who were around me, was that I would have "terrible" penmanship because I was left handed. So it was imperative for me to learn how to type; and so I did, even excel in typing at least. (ya lunch and recess to, ha ha) My professor was so proud of my accomplishments on the "keyboard" when I hit 85 words per minute 95% accuracy that I actually pulled out an A, in something. (We-uh whew!)

Our food in the cafeteria, was just O K and that was as far as it goes. But we did have an annual food fight in this big huge, old cafeteria building, which stood all by itself, and the ceiling was very high, but some mash potatoes would still get stuck up there. *School discipline* was "no one could leave campus for two days. (Aw-Shucks.)

All my other classes through high-school were pretty normal & quite mundane, & being the "genius" I am, I pulled close to a 3 point G.P.A. through-out high-school, but let me tell you it wasn't easy, there was a lot of tests & loads of homework to do, and as I said, they would Not grade on a curve. But back then, they still gave out GRADES! Like A-B-C-D-F. Okay Okay, I know that you "young'ins" don't know anything about that sort of grading today, anymore.

Who Got Who?

One bright comfortable sunny day, I was walking back from downtown Milwaukee, (our school was about 30 some blocks west of the main part of Milwaukee—at the time) when 3 other teenagers about 14-ish (one was on a bicycle) walking towards me, then actually approached me and two of them grabbed my arms and the third demanded my wallet and watch or else they were going to beat me to a "pulp". Well that was interesting, cause I gave them what I had in my wallet, and pockets (about a buck or two total), I had no money in the wallet-no credit-card-no drivers-license, (come on, I was 14, and this was 1964) then they quickly took off. But here is where *Your Hero* shines through, (ya). I had, just a few weeks earlier bought a nice leather belt, with a zippered, secret compartment on the inside, & they weren't the wiser. So I kept my rare & valuable (at the time) $20.00 bill, that Hank gave me, in there. (Ah Ha!) So I felt quite relieved & vindicated, much less thankful that I didn't get beat up too. smithereens.

Yes, I was a swim team member, (Surprise!) first I made J.V. And then later I even got to Varsity as a Quarto (junior-four), & I did well in the 50 yard & relays. (remember those biceps) We had a really nice pool and we even had a standard, and a high diving board. I was getting pretty good on both of them too, just not well enough to compete. My physique wasn't/isn't pretty. (Ya I know the candy as a kid) But just try to find a high-school with a high dive board, now-a-days. Insurance companies will no longer cover such liabilities.

The BUCK Stops Where?

We had a nice gymnasium which had a lot a seats for fans. When Milwaukee got its "brand new" professional basketball team, (they didn't even have their name yet, now known as the Milwaukee BUCKS) practiced at our gym. Guess who we got to see practice there every day? Uh Huh? Yup! The real Lou Al Sindor, *aka* Kareem-Abdul-Jabbar. Yes he did! The funniest part was, he even showered in line, with the rest of us students (all guys-remember). But I reflect on how he had to duck down in our locker/shower, because the ceilings just weren't made "quite" high enough, for him. Awe.

The last day of "finals "came in 1968 in early to mid-December. My parents came to pick me up for Christmas break, but before we went home, we continued down the "Rock" freeway towards

Janesville, WI., where there was a nice ski hill, at least in southern Wisconsin, (we're not known for our mountains) my mom, dad, and I went "downhill" snow skiing.

Being that, we were all pretty novice at this whole thing, we started at the bunny hill. We had gone skiing, maybe two or three times before. After we had taken some really "fun" runs down one of three full size downhills; I went "zooming" down and at the base I waited and waited at the base for my parents. Now I must say the the snow certainly wasn't deep, we had just started getting cold weather, and a couple of small snow storms, but they had been making snow a lot, and it was all pretty good.

I waited for about five minutes, then took the cable chair back up. When I arrived at the top, I got off and turned to see my mom standing over my dad, about a third of the way down the hill. "NOW What! I questioned. So I raced down to them as fast as I could, just then a "ski patrol" woman came down closer to the woods, and stopped by us too.

My dad could **not move**, he was on his back, and the lady used her walky-talky to call for a stretcher to come down by us. Meanwhile she and I looked around to see what may have been the cause of dads fall. We were well within the snow-run and about six-eight feet from the tree line.

Suddenly I spotted something in the snow, and reached down to brush it off, and the patrol lady came when I announced my find. It was a big piece of solid concrete about two 'x two' x eight" high, slightly snow covered . . . It was laying right in line with all of the skiers coming down the right hand side of the slope. She and I picked it up and threw it into the woods. That's right, my dad had broken his back.

Dad was laid up for a long time in the hospital and then at home. A year later my parents sued for the financial damages, and got "ZIP, Zilch, Nada, at all. The judge ruled that the accident was caused by an "unforeseen incident". Wait! Was that a sign of things to come?

After the first semester of my freshman college grade (Duo) we had it arranged that we go on an "adventure" journey to Mexico as a class. We **did** have girls (now) in college. And they knew that I sold "pop-up" campers, so the school bought 6 of them and about 20 of us 15 guys 5 girls and six chaperones and professor all drove down during our 1 month hiatus).

The taxi driver had to go back through the city, and he was driving down those city streets at about 45-50 and "zooming" through all of the red lights. Yes we were all starting to get into a panic, and asked him to turn on his headlights and slowdown. Believe it or not he told us that he couldn't, "out of respect" for the other drivers. WHAT? He said, that down there, they don't want to "blind" each other with their headlights, and that the stop and go lights were really only for the daytime. Speed limits didn't really count, since there were no police watching speeds. So, we did make it, and we got through Mexico City, really quick.

All went well driving down to Mexico City. We (five of us) fellas, rented a cab to go for a "joy ride" and check out some of the night life. About 10-10:30 pm we hailed down another taxi, to take us to the edge of town, back to your camp-ground.

We even traveled all the way to Acapulco. 5 of us guys rented a fishing charter; to go "catch the big ones" Well we did, three of the guys all caught something, as we took turns (two at a time) two guys caught swordfish one got a tarpon, and when it was my turn, I didn't just catch a sailfish, but after a 45 minute battle. (I'm serious) we were finally able to get it up to behind the boat. The captain suddenly realized, why I seemed so weak in pulling it in. The sailfish was being chased by a shark, and it was putting double its power in avoiding, attacking shark below the surfaced.

When I was finally able to get it, just below the back of the boat, the captain took his pistol out and when the shark came close to the surface, he shot it. I was able to land that beauty, quick after that. That's where things got even more interesting.

How true? Back then who knows? We college kids didn't know better, but the captain said that we HAD to keep the Sailfish, out of some Mexican sea-fish law. Any more than three caught, the rest had to be taken in and paid for. (ya–right) But hey, what were we going to do? We're in the Pacific ocean on his boat, and we had to get back to shore. So I got "stuck" bringing in a 6' 120 lb. sailfish that I now had to pay for too. (with what–my good looks?)

When we got ashore, I had to pay $125.00, to have it stuffed and shipped. I had about $40.00 left to get back home; now what? Yup, find a telephone (that worked) and what else {call Hank}. He said that he would wire the money to a bank down there, and Yes *thankfully* he did. (we hoped) Exactly 6 months later the "now" mounted Sailfish arrived in Milwaukee Arrived!

We hung it (the sailfish–of course) over the office area of our showroom for over 25 years. It was beautiful and quite a conversation piece. (And the best part is that I didn't have to talk about the one that "got away.)

Chap. 4

No Sex Ed.—No Drivers Ed.

I became sixteen as a Junior—(Quarto) at Concordia High, in November of 1966. And guess what kids, I was able to take my driver's test, on the day of my birthday, there was NO "drivers-ed." back then (whew hew), and yes we did have cars, (even back then) that were enclosed, too. My dad drove me to the testing station. And of course, the way my life goes, that had some interesting events too. You see where I had to take the test, they didn't have curbs out there yet, so they used a great big long telephone pole and they laid it on the edge of the gravel parking lot. And I had to get my mother's '61 Chevy Impala up next to it, not to close and not too far away, but "juusst right." Oh, that was a real challenge. And of course, as you would expect, I didn't pass the first time that I took it. The examiner said that I didn't turn my head far enough when I did my "Y" turns. So after ten days I went back and "Yesss", I DID pass! The examiner had to make sure that I was close enough, yet not to close to the long electric pole, so he had to try to open the passenger door, but the pole laid to high and the door wouldn't open, so that's how he calibrated the distance from the "curb". Cute huh?

Now, that summer was the time that Wisconsin had just introduced motorcycle safety training and I hadn't driven a motorcycle yet in my life, but I sure did a lot of snowmobiling, and like I said earlier, Atv's weren't "invented" yet. So my dad told the clerk that I would like my cycle validation also, the man behind the counter looked at me and then my dad and said, "He just passed his driver's license test 10 minutes ago, I'm holding the application in my hand, how on earth did he put at least 500 miles on a cycle that quick, and here in the middle of November, besides?"

My dad simply looked the clerk in the eye, and said," He has been riding vehicles "off road" a lot, for years now, doesn't that count too?" The man just shook his head and took the money and stamped my application, and we left. Thanks Dad. Now you ask, what's the big deal of getting the cycle validation, so important? Just wait and see, you'll love this part too.

Right after that, I started going down to Hank's gas station whenever I could, to clean up and help out. When I was up in the city at school I just had to take a long ride on the city bus, down to the limits, and I had to make sure that I had a dime, on me, to call up, when I got down there, and he would send somebody up a couple of miles north to pick me up. But hey "all that" to hang around a bunch of greasy auto mechanics. (two or three) In all of my spare time, that's where I could be found. I did learn a little about mechanics; And Death again, as well. What? You Say? Let me explain.

They changed a lot of car and semi-truck tires in the garage part, and they would have to use big sledge hammers and wedges, into the truck tires to break the release bar, change the tire, put it back in place, and pump it up. Back then it wasn't any kind of law yet, but Hank would even warn me to stay in the inner door-way, when I saw them trying to fill up a semi-tire (no it's not part of a tire, but a tire for a semi-truck . . . Okay?) If the locking ring didn't "hold", it could and would blow off. This ring is about three feet across, and about an inch wide and a half inch thick. It was very heavy spring steel, and it took a lot of work to try to get it locked into the edge of the rim. Well I was watching one of the experienced mechanics airing up a brand new (semi-truck) tire—better? And he didn't put the ring down, facing the ground, because the inlet valve had to be facing him. He's just about got it filled all of the way when **B A M**, the ring blew off, and crushed his ribs, and legs, **KILLING** Him

30

Instantly; while I was watching. Certainty of death, is All around; YOU BET!

Trying to stay on Track

Here we go, now back home, by all of the inland lakes near my parents' home, it was the *dead* (get it dead) of winter in January of '67, lots of ice & snow, and Hank had now taken on that brand of snowmobiles called Trade Winds, *Tigers*. He bought 3 to be a dealer. Two 9 hp, and one "super killer" 11 hp model. Look in 1967 these were "hot", ya, and now "weed-eaters" have more power. Well there was a race a couple miles from our house, and I convinced my parents and Hank, that I could really help get some publicity, so people would know that we are selling this new brand of snowmobiles. So they let me enter the race, on the lake, called *Big Muskeg*o. The track was just on the raw ice, and about the size of a football field, in the round.

I was bundled up, helmet on (2/3s model), with a stocking cap, some knit mitts, and I was wearing a brand new Trade Winds bright orange cold weather jacket. Let me tell you, I felt like I was really some "hot stuff". I sure wished the jackets back then could really make me feel hot, much less even warm.

All eight of us that were in our class, pulled up on the starting line aaannddd the flag dropped and we all took off, no carbides, no studs on the track, just the "will to win" and freeze while doing so. After the first lap I wasn't dead last, just third from the end, but let me tell you, that by the second lap I was so far behind everybody else, that the flying snow that blinded all of us that were racing, was even settling. But I put my whole heart into it, and after the fifth lap, I only was about a full two or three laps behind everyone. Ice fishermen could have fished there, I was so slow.

Hey Now Look; I Did get the attention, and recognition for our new brand of snowmobile, but it wasn't the good kind, for me or for what any of us wanted or was hoping for, especially when the announcer told everyone to be quiet, because it looked like I was trying to take a nap. It was so humiliating, to say the least. I just melted into the snowbank, till spring. I think they found my bright orange jacket to get me out. Anybody see a "pattern" here?

"C" I told Ya!

Spring and summer went well, and I got a lot of swimming and fishing in at the lake, then fall came around and I started my junior year in high-school. That's when our friend Hank, one day, stuck his finger into my nose then smiled and said "You get straight B's or better and I'll get you a Honda 50!" "What? Wow! Really?" I screeched, and put all my effort in doing well in school. Realize, that is like telling a kid nowadays you'd get him a Sportster, or 250 Ninja or the like.

As life would have it, I wasn't quite smart enough (ya, I knew you saw that already) to pull off straight B's or better. I did get one "C". Ouch, that hurt so badly. So my B's & one C, didn't drive me into despondence, but now I was not able to get a Honda 50, that really did hurt. Oh well I did try. I guess it just wasn't "meant to be". Yet—that is. (here comes Providence-just wait No not the insurance company)

This snowmobile sales thing, started going a bit, and then we got a couple of Trade Winds "pop-up" campers in and before you know it, we sold one of them also. There still wasn't anything about motorcycles in our lives, yet, but as I shared earlier My dreams were almost crushed. Then one Saturday in fall of 1966 my parents and I went to the Truck stop, to help Hank straighten up around the place.

My mom and dad would often go in and help Hank do his paper work, which was definitely NOT his thing. He would occasionally repeat too many of us around him that he had gotten through his first year of high-school, and that was it. And then tell us how he just worked on the farm, 'till the war started and he enlisted, which he was put into the Sea Bee's because he was very mechanically adept, and knew and understood engines very well. I really think he told us that over and over again, out of pride, not for sympathy. Because he really was quite successful, anyway.

As it turned out, that was the best "C" I ever got. How Sweet— really it was. Can we all say Providence again? (OK maybe not yet) The worst part is, I still can't spell Trigonometry???, much less do it. But wait the best is yet to come from all of this, you'll see. The story, keeps getting better, and I do hope you will all recognize that I am a firm believer in this "concept" called, "*providence*". Merriam Webster definition: "divine guidance and care". Just wait.

My mom, dad and I, went to the gas station to help Hank. That's when he walked up toward me with a great big "Santa Claus" grin on his face, he motioned us to come into the station and he flailed his arm past the two motor-bikes and said, "What do ya think? Some guys came into the station and told me to come to a presentation about a new motorcycle that just came to America; so I went to Janesville, (Wi.) last Wednesday and took a look around and got a nice big free meal and all the drinks I wanted." He continued, "I didn't know what I had done, but I got one heck of a hangover, and drove back to Oak Creek with a real {whopper} of a buzz in my head . . ." (We don't condone that-of course)

Do They Really Roll?

"A few days later they called and told me to come back down to Janesville, and pick up the bikes I just bought. I said {What bikes?}" Hank blurted out. "Hey look, you signed the dealer agreement, so come and get them, they're here, now." On a drunk, I became an official Kawasaki dealer. "What?" I hollered out again? A WHAT-dealer?" "Kawasaki" was the reply from the distributor's voice. "Your bikes are waiting, for you to come pick them up".

"So I drove back down there with the old flat stake truck that wouldn't go into reverse, and sure enough three big wooden crates were just sitting there. "Let's get them loaded up so I can get back to Milwaukee." Hank demanded. That was part of the problem too, as they told him, all we've got in this warehouse is this old forklift, and it does go up and down, but it won't go forward or backward." So they had to push the forklift to the back of the old midsized stake truck, which they had to push down the loading ramp to get the bikes out of the warehouse. Pretty "Hi-Tech; eh?"

With a big grin on his face he proudly said "And so here they are." Hank gloated, still with a super headache. At that point he now became one of the very first Kawasaki dealers in the United States.

My dad asked Hank. "What the heck are these things, and who's going to buy something that you can't even pronounce the name of?" My dad asked Hank. "Well, I promised Dave a Honda 50, and this seemed to be an even better one, it's an 85 cc and the other is a new C2SS 120. Pretty cool, eh?" he proudly announced again.

"Yes! But David did Not get all B's!" my mother quickly snapped back. "I know, I know, but he really tried hard, didn't YOU?" turning to me inquisitively. "I suppose, but whose going to teach him how to drive this silly thing?" my mom then asked. "The guys from the distributor showed me how, and I think I can figure it out, to show him." came back-hopefully.

Then my dad chimed in "Hank don't you need a license to sell these things?" Ya, I guess so; Don. Maybe you could help, by taking the test ahead of me, and save the answers; Okay?" So my dad went to the State Motor Vehicle dept. and studied the "Being a Dealer" guide, and then a few days later went back and took the test. And he even PASSED!

Now, it was Hank's turn, a few days later, he went down and took the test, and instead of "failing miserably" he kept the answers that my dad had given him, and after the second try He Passed Too! Sorta . . . But now at least, we Are official Motorcycle Dealers.

And that unlikely event, allowed us to become the start of a lot of my life's adventures. Unbeknown to us at the time again, we had just become the 17th Kawasaki dealer in the whole United States of

America. We sold them under the company name of Oak Creek Towing. And I was completely enthralled with the whole ordeal. "Man, life couldn't get much cooler than that;" So I thought.

Hank showed me how to use the clutch and twist-grip throttle. And there was that funny little shift-lever, down on the left side of the motor. It was GREAT fun riding around the big truck parking lot. Then one day, Hank and my dad let me go out on the little cross road. I'm telling you this, because, the road in front of the truck stop/gas-station was the original major arterial that took a person from the Upper peninsula of Michigan to Miami Florida. See the interstate still hadn't come all the way through quite yet to us so any and all traffic came right by the station and our new "toy" store. The front of a gas station was all it was, but hey it was a start.

Things kept getting better and better, with sales and people who bought everything back then with cash, (an occasional check, but realize almost none of these vehicles was over a $1000.00 The 85 cc bikes was $299.00 and the brand new model 120 was $375. (That's true I'm not joking)

Later on then came the other new models; Holy Kaw! (see–it's coming) they were unbelievable. A big new Samurai 250 2 cylinder, and the chrome paneled gas tank 350 cc Avenger. And then later, we even *hesitantly* bought and got in an "unbelievable" motorcycle; a huge new W2SS two cylinder four stroke 650 cc monster, with twin carburetors. (look out BSA and Triumph-here we come)

Strangest thing, was that the little space in the gas station was now gone, and customers could barely even get in, much less use the men's room. That boat company Carver, that Hank had built the building for a few years earlier, was expanding so fast that they too needed more room. They came to Hank and said that they were moving out to a new facility that they had just bought and built a new building on. So now Hank was without a tenant . . . hmmm, see anything coming?

In 1971 we entered an annual spring consumer show that was called The Milwaukee Sentinel Sport Travel and Boat Show. It ran for a 10 day period, every March, and always right around St. Patrick's Day. It was always strongly attended by thousands and thousands. It originally took place in two separate convention halls that were attached, right in downtown Milwaukee. We were new and little, compared to the big boat & motor companies, so they gave us an eight x eight' square at the bottom of the staircase in the oldest building. Hey, we thought this isn't all that bad, a good number of folks should still see us hopefully, at least those that could at least climb the stairs. (See, We "yuppies" could all still get around pretty well back then.) {hee-hee} And we were the only motorcycle display there. (marketing?)

We stuffed eight or nine bikes on the floor and on display, with no room for even a chair or table. We were there in the spring of 73 when I had just come to find out that I needed a lot more Bible knowledge. Because, let's face it, eight years just wasn't enough. I went every day from open to close 9-9, and talked my little "head off," about how wonderful these new bikes were that we are "now" selling. You'll never believe this, but back then, most people who walked up to the booth, couldn't even pronounce Kawasaki. They'd go, "What the heck are these. Where are these things made?" We still were not a very "enlightened" nation back then yet. Hank would just say "south side Hawaiian" and they all nodded smiled.

__Word;__ be Gone

On one of those days, a customer who was standing in one of the corners was looking at a certain model, so while I was in the middle of the booth, reading my Bible (you'll see why, real soon), between customer contacts, this person motioned for me to come over. So I set my Bible down on the top of the seat of another motorcycle, that was a little closer to the rope/railing we had going around the columns of the booth. I joyfully and enthusiastically answered the questions that the customer had about the bike, and I invited him to come down to our store, to check them out even closer. He nodded and thanked me for my help, and kept walking along. So I turned and went back to the bike in the middle, to keep reading, I looked on the seat, then the floor, and all around the bike that I had put my Bible on, and I realized that it wasn't there. It had been STOLEN! I had been given that by my parents for my Lutheran confirmation and it was a *Thomas Nelson*, leather-bound gold trimmed and full of notes that I had taken over the years. It's Now GONE!

My immediate thoughts were "Who would steal a Bible?" Then "that little voice" we hear so much about, said to me "They needed worse than You." 'nuff said, I thought and hummed to myself the rest of my free time, that day.

Just going a little farther with that *"Bible Thing"* As a little aside. I have to tell you that a few years later, I was invited down to a pastors conference and what I learned from this seminar down in Wheaten, Ill. Impacted me greatly through life. A man named Bill Gothard was speaking, to all of us clergy, and at about half way through, he introduced his very *very* senior father who had been the president of the *Gideon Bible Society* in the '40's. He told us things that I never forgot and to me, it was just astounding.

Right after World War II, he (the senior Gothard) had received a phone call from General Douglas MacArthur, who asked him to provide to the U.S. Government 1 million Bibles (printed in Japanese) and one thousand missionaries that spoke Japanese.

He immediately replied to the general "Yes Sir. I can get you the Bibles, but sir, Japan is a civilized nation, we don't have missionaries learning to speak Japanese. Why would you want a thousand missionaries for Japan?"

The general insistently responded with a spectacular appendage. "We have studied the Japanese culture to as far back as possible, and it has become clear that whenever the Japanese nation fought another and conquered that other nation, they required the other people to worship their god, Buddha.

But, whenever the Japanese fought and lost to another country, they would *take on* the god of that nation. We are expecting them to take on the God of the Bible, so we need the Bibles, and missionaries to go over there to minister to them." "I'll do **All** I can," came the heart pounding reply from senior Mr. Gothard.

That was very dramatic. But now think about it for a minute. After W.W.II, the great "boon" in society came through the whole American economy from the 50's to mid-90 at least. We were on one heck of a grand "buying spree"; a parade of self-indulgence, be it in the house, garage, yard, or trailer, maybe even motorcycles.

America had started on one heck of a "spending binge." We were "blowing" money like water, and then we got into the whole "credit" thing, and guess who supplied a lot of our purchases—JAPAN! NO, Not China-or Korea . . . Yet! Yes, because they had lost the war; they took on our "god," pure and simple—Materialism! Ya-Y a, I don't sound like a "good-ole-American boy," right now, do I? Lovin' all that "Jap Crap." *That came at me a lot,* in those days. Well you're WRONG if you think that I don't really love this, My country, and what it stands for, and I even proclaim it worldwide, when talking to executives and others. The Bible has a little word though for, that kind of god . . . it's called _Mammon_.!

What IS REALLY Important to US? Remember . . . *You AIN'T* taking anything with you on your last journey.

Chap. 5

"Let the Good Times Roll!

Back now in '67 again. The bikes just sat there for a few months. Remember it was November, but the distributor from the small town just south of Madison, WI. Also carried a brand new make of snowmobile called the FoxTrac, and they convinced Hank to become a Fox Trac dealer, then too.

We did sell seven or eight of them that winter. But no cycles, yet or pop-up campers; either. It was a good thing Hank had his diesel sales, and truck scale to keep "the lights on", for us.

Spring of 1968 came along and people were *starting to stop* (cute huh?) in and see all of the "big-boy" toys, that we had on the floor. And everybody, was curious about these strange new little 2 stroke Japanese motorcycles.

After graduation, it was almost a given that I was probably *now* going to keep pursuing this whole "religious churchy" thing, so that fall I was right back there, but now in the new class-room building reserved only for the college students. Strange as this might sound and kind of weird, even for me, but after the first week, I found myself liking classical Greek, the most. {I really have no idea why} maybe just because it was as kind-of-weird as I was/am}? But I did learn to *luv* Baklava a delicious Greek pastry desert. (close to frozen custard-you'll see)

Yes, every parents "worst" nightmare." I committed. I had gone to a week-long camp between eighth-grade and high-school to

39

learn how to play the trumpet. I'm just not a good "pucker-err?
It was OK, but as you'll see later I took after my two aunts. (No,
not in their clothes or make up-please) The most awesome musical
instrument. The DRUM's! See, what I liked about reading music
for drums, is that those cute little notes are all on the same line. (So
much easier). Not Really, but still true. I found a used set of *Ludwig*
{Pink Champagne} double tom, single bass, and a metal chrome
snare drum, in the classifieds, and I just had to get 'em. So I set them
up in the basement, to practice for the summer. Sorry Mom & Dad.
(Don and Joyce, were never the same)

In fall, I did have to drive to & from school each day, for those
two years, of college in Milwaukee. Because I didn't live at the
college dorm on campus, or an apartment off campus. I lived at home
with my parents; but hey no room & board or rent, so why not, At
least I was paying my own tuition now, No student loans, just work,
when not in class. It was about 20 miles each way {not so bad, when
gas cost [before Jimmy Carters oil embargo] .19 cents a gallon. Yes!
I'm Not kidding, really that was it. So all in all, my life was pretty
sedate for a young adult; especially in the late sixties & early '70's.
We didn't even have any kind of graduation from "Junior College"
just went home and stayed.

I'm now getting ready to finish my college days in Milwaukee,
so now, which city should I go to, for my final college years? This
is where it starts getting even more interesting; you'll see; No really
it does. Heard that before, huh? My school-mate friend and buddy,
Rick (for most of the last 4 years in high-school & Jr. College),
& I, vacillated (Yes that's a clean word) about which was the next
direction we would take in our educational adventure in the whole
Concordia system. We were now qualified to go to Seminary in
St. Louis, Mo. or St. Paul, MN. or else we could go to Valparaiso
Indiana, or the Teacher's college just down in River Forest, Illinois.
See our high school classes qualified us for being like now—days
"A.P." Courses. (German, Latin, Music etc.)

We decided to go down to R.F. to finish up our Bachelors. The weirdest thing about Concordia River Forest, was that they had "tri-mesters" instead of semesters. So it took three sessions to get through the course, but what it did offer, was a 4th "tri-mester" session (ya a 4th of a tri?) during the summer, so you could either "catch-back-up" or progress ahead, in some courses. That was kind of cool.

We "hooked" on to another co-student, that we knew, but he was a nice guy just kind of a "geek" (and that was before computers) and we let him join us in our "apartment search. We needed all the help we could get to keep our rent as livable as we each could afford.

So for our first year, we found a small apartment on the 3rd floor—no elevator, right near the intersection of Harlem and Lake St, in Oak Park Ill. It was about 10-12 blocks from school.

We worked all kinds of part-time jobs, down there, like filling little plastic bags with topsoil. I even got a janitorial position at one of the suburbs police dept. /jail. Pulling used "hypos" out from under the jail cell bench was real common. Now this was one of my biggest regrets down there. The village of Forest Park, whose police station I worked at, had a '49 Hardly tank shifter police trike that they never really used. (maybe sometimes for parades) They would have sold it to me for about $1800.00, (which I didn't have) but, WOW in 2003, H.D.'s 100th birthday, and that bike was like brand new, would that have brought in some "big coin" for me? But oh well,;;; me buy a Hardley? Naaaaa.

just quit the wining!

The three of us were pretty good college kids. We even had a cat, named "Drizzles" (yes he was properly named, and had some issues). Once, my roommate decided that we were going to start making our own wine, so we bought a big green glass jug, some yeast and sugar and oh *ya*, even grapes, and we put a balloon on the top so we could keep tract (today-monitor) the progress the yeast was making. A few

41

weeks later, we all had a longer weekend that we stayed back up in Milwaukee, and when we got back to the third floor apartment, a lot later than normal. To our surprise discovered the whole white painted kitchen, was now adorned with splattered purple. OH-Ya, it was a great time trying to clean up. What fun! That's right . . . the big green wine bottle fell off the high upper shelf and splattered green shards of broken glass pieces all over. See the balloon "neutralizer" had gotten so big it burst against the wall, and ceiling and down went the jug.

Our second year, down in River Forest, was full of incredible events that I know, will keep you very intently reading. We had another class-mate back in Wisconsin, who was a bit more "daring" than we three. My roommate/classmate Rick and I, took the invitation to move in just down the block in the suburb of Forest Park where I had been working. That town was just "kitty corner" from Oak Park, and across the street from River Forest, Ill. This was a very old 2 story bungalow that had been made into 2 one-room apartments upstairs and we had all of the rest of the downstairs to ourselves. That's the clue . . . who is "ourselves"? This old house was right on the "main drag" & it was a very busy city street in the near-west side of Chicago cluster of suburbs.

Try to picture this house, just a half block south of this rather busy larger older grocery store chain, and then next to that was a muffler/brake repair 4 garage doors; just south of that was an alley which was the old drive way for this old house's backyard that was now all paved. It came across as an alley all the way to the next block. Now right behind the house was a fully paved parking lot for the veterinary clinic behind us, there was room for about six-eight cars. With another exit/entrance to the cross street south of the house; but "oh ya" just immediately south of the old house we were now living in, was a corner bar, which was heavily frequented by fellas that preferred other fellas; (was that P.C. Enough?) NO. I'm Not studying to be a realtor. Just wait. Here it comes.

"hello, I love You . . . Your My Man . . . please tell me your name"

Here is the unusual part. The bar across the street, from that "guys" bar on the same side of the major road was a true blue full-fledged "biker-bar". It was always interesting, outside on the two corners, when the patrons would leave. The part that truly enlightened me, was once a big "burly" bearded kind of guy, who was very ruff, gruff, coat, vested biker, with many colors on his vest stepped out of the biker bar.

I saw him walk across the street, to the "other" bar, just when another fella stepped out of the doorway, the two guys, were "shall we say, "physically enjoying each other's company" all over each other. Then they crossed back over the street and got on that biker's chopper, and for lack of more room, they "snugly" took off, with the rider holding on to the drivers body parts. I was just sitting on the porch on that nice evening, realizing that I still had a lot to learn about life. Yes "LOLA" by the Kinks, had just come out. (freaky)

Like I said, there were two small single room apartments up stairs, of this big old house, where two different "oldsters" lived each on their own. They had to climb a rather rickety old wooden stairs that went up the back to an outside walkway to either room. We rarely got to see either one of the little old men that were renting, each of those rooms. We did hear from them a lot, in the evenings though, when a large gathering of guys and gals, would hang out in our "black room" with Jimi Hendrix, or the Doors were cranked loud. All the posters on the ceilings and walls, almost seemed to "come to life" in that totally black lite "full quad" audio room. It would go late into the night, and these guys upstairs, couldn't get any sleep. Maybe that's why I still feel guilty over what you'll see, just happened next.

Rick and I moved over to that place together. (The other guy chose to live in a dorm after the first year). As I've said, Rick and I were friends and he even sometimes took my cycle to school, because he had some early morning classes, and it was so quick and easy to park. Then he'd be back by the time I needed it. It was parked out back behind the house too, right by my car.

Till death do us part?

Early one morning, (maybe around nine or so) I suddenly awoke from the flashing slit of light coming in from the outside window, below the shade, and I heard a group of voices. I instantly became awake, and when I realized that a bright red light really was flashing in my eyes. My first reaction was "Oh No, Rick had an accident on the bike, or something is happening to my beautiful pastel yellow car, I hope nobody slashed the tires, or hit the car. But just what could have happened? I ran out into the parking lot, just with my briefs on, (now you know-they're not boxers) and I was suddenly seeing a large group of police; all around my *gorgeous* 1969 black vinyl top pastel Yellow Chevy Nova with the 2 wide-outlined black racing stripes that I had just painted, on the back trunk deck like the wide bordered GM *SS* stripes.

My gut sank; "what's going on here?" Was my anxious question to one of the cops, who immediately stuck his baton-ed arm out and hollered "get away kid?" I jumped and motioned while screeching "hey That's MY CAR! What's Going ON, over there?" "I told you. Get Away from here, Now!" Then another officer asked. "Do you know this guy?" "Oh No?" My heart just plummeted down, it had to be my good friend Rick. Oh please let him not be hurt or killed, PLEASE! Nervously walking over to the front of my car by the driver's door, I saw a couple of officers, squatted down right in front of my four—wheeled beauty, now strangely, instead of a classy pastel yellow. There was a dead man laying right in front of my car. Where he had just swallowed his shot gun, and pulled the trigger. You can just imagine what was "All over" the front and top of my sweet soft yellow car.

What was left of his head, was still up against my front bumper. "Thank GOD" it wasn't Rick or anyone that I knew personally, well. But I did realize that it was one of the old men who lived up-stairs. (See my guilt?)

Again I heard, "Get away from here." "But that's my car!" I said again. "So, Do you know him?" I was asked again, and I said that I knew that he lived upstairs, & that was all. "What Happened? I cried out. "He couldn't take life anymore kid, and ended "it all" right in front of your car. Ya, my beautiful yellow car, "But; **THAT's** My Car!" I blurted out again. "Not Right Now, kid" "Just go back into the house, till we come for you." another cop told me. Let me tell you . . . Now that was One horrifying morning in Forest Park, Ill. For me, that I certainly will never forget. That was some more life trauma that I sure wasn't ready for. It seemed like death was just following me everywhere.

As another little aside; Rick and I got a few jobs each semester to play in some bands, and that usually paid just enough to get us the gas money to go to work the gig. But we sure loved playing the few gigs we did get. Rick was an absolutely incredible guitar player. And that was another big blunder on my part. In all those years I never thought to have him show me how to play the guitar. And he could almost rivaled Clapton and Hendrix (at least, I thought so).

He was so talented, with that 6 string electric that the music flowed so great when he played. Rick said to me one time, after going out with the girl from Milwaukee, who was now going to the same school as he and I, down in River Forest, "Dave, you know that she's got a sister just a couple of years younger. Maybe you could go out with her sometime. "Who knows maybe, I'll marry Jen, and you marry her sister, and we'd even be brother-in-laws." (ha ha ha- guess what)

Later on, in that school year . . . real close to my "hopeful" graduation which was in March of all times, I finally agreed to go with my two roommates {Rick and Wayne} and their girlfriends who kept pestering me to join them on any Wednesday night to go to this so called "rap" session, that a little old lady had going on in the basement of a two story duplex closer to downtown Chicago. Now do you see why I stalled? So finally the week before I was supposed to graduate, in March 1972, I gave in, and went, (because of my deeply spiritual desire-rightttt). Truth is, the one distant roommate Wayne, who I had just gotten to know a little bit that year, *convinced me with these heavy spiritual words*—"there's a lot of really cool *chicks* there". So {somehow} I finally agreed to go; it wasn't too hard. Pretty deep-huh?

See, I told you how spiritual I was . . . ya right. But here I must share, how the Concordia system, mostly in Milwaukee, and the six tri-mesters worth of schooling, in River Forest, did give me a real huge leap forward in my upcoming work years.

What was that? You might say. Well this might really sound strange at first, but please let me explain, so you too see the **value**, like I, finally did. We, students at Concordia, had to take 6 semesters of Psychology! What? To be a Lutheran pastor? Yes! See Psychology isn't changing people's minds like Psychiatry is, but rather just better understanding people's ways of thinking, from their emotions, to their cultural variances, and their up-bringing. That's why I became so interested in traveling all around the world, it's so valuable just to learn about different cultural differences, that helps make us think the way we do, about ourselves, others and life in general. Here's a quick paradigm.

Sink or swim

If a huge cruise-ship sinks and there's only enough room in the cold Alaska waters (not Titanic) for each life boat to hold 10 people, who gets in the boat, and who has to stay in the cold water and be left behind? The *old*, the little *babes*, the *rich*, the *poorer*, the *healthy*? YOU DECIDE! See my point? And, now why, do you say who should get in, and who must stay in the freezing water?

All of this, being said right here, because I was going to use my "deep" (ya right) Psychological training in this up and coming environment; especially if somebody tries to maneuver me in their "strange" thoughts. So here we Go . . .

Chap. 6

How to "Control Eternity"

Actually, now here is where my real story starts . . . Really, so far it's just been building to this point. Get <u>READY</u>! No, I'm not kidding, really I'm not. Awe, come on believe me, please . . . I know you've heard it before, but it is true!

Yes, I finally went to this Chicago bungalow, with my room-mates and their girlfriends. I had to drive, because after this so-called "rap" session I was going to head right back up to Milwaukee that night. We parked out on a quiet residential street, rowed with houses. We "quietly" walked down one of the sidewalks that was between the houses, and into the back-yard, then around a corner and down a short set of wooden steps; we opened the door to the basement, and "Holy Kaw" (you'll get more later) the basement was packed full of young adults (later high-school & some college) age, like us, the "oh so *"wise"* ones." There were six or seven long church type banquet tables and a coffee pot, plus a "fridge" in the corner, and everyone was "chit-chatting away, while drinking their coffee or soda (that's what we call it in Wisconsin/ not "pop).

Just about 8:00 o-clock in the evening, this senior lady dressed in a sweatshirt, and blue jeans, came down the basement stairs from the middle of the house. She was a home maker, grandma, and years earlier, her and her husband were missionaries with *New Tribes Bible Institute*. In the 50's & 60's. She served with her husband Don, in South America, close to the middle of the continent.

Igua-what?

This missionary couple, Don and Lois Peterson, and their kids, were "stationed" in *Asuncion*, Paraguay, near the Iguazu waterfalls, being in the central part of South America it is one of the oldest cities on the whole continent, but oh how far back in the jungle it is. It isn't much bigger than a small town that we would picture. But that was where you had to get all your supplies, just to live. A far cry from bustling Chicago, that's for sure.

When she spoke she was very lucid, vocal, descriptive and energetic, and passionate, with the words she read from the Bible, and then expounded on individual verses. Not interpreting them but putting them into a more modern day contextual understanding, so we could relate to the writers better.

She spoke for little over an hour. Then everyone broke up and started talking with each other again. I didn't really know anyone there, except those that brought me, so I just sat and sipped my coffee. I was struck by the fact that the **ambiance** was so absorbing and almost affecting ones demeanor. There was such an "air" of joy, and camaraderie amongst everyone there. In and of itself this was rather electrifying, to me. Wanna hear the best part? There were NO drugs, alcohol or other stimulants beside coffee and soda, either.

This is now, maybe the second or third cup of coffee that I had ever drank so far in my entire life; but I had to drive back to Milwaukee, that night, so I figured it might just help. The weirdest thing is since then, I drink about four-five large cups of coffee per day, and to me it doesn't matter if it's hot or cold, (or even just lukewarm). Some say Uuch . . .

In a few minutes, shortly after I had just been sitting by myself, the "rap session" teacher-lady came and sat across from me and introduced herself. "Hi; I'm <u>Lois Peterson</u>, and you are Dave?" Now I can be cordial and share conversation with almost anybody, but for some strange reason she "almost" intimidated me into silence, so I just nodded positively. Not by expression, or words, but just by her presence and aura. See, after listening to her talk in the "class", I knew that she was much *much* wiser than her apparel would suggest, otherwise she appeared as a nice little lady who takes care of the house, and maybe grand kids.

Here now are her words, with questions and comments to me that *forever changed* my life and the course of eternity for me and many others over my life-time. If you pay close attention, it may just have that affect and *"eternal change"* for you, too.

"So what did you think of class tonight?" She asked. "It was good," I cordially replied, quickly. "Oh, so you know something about the Bible, then?" She asked. "Yes, I am graduating from Concordia River Forest, next week {unless I flunk all my finals}" I like to insert a bit of "comic relief" (never would have guessed, would you). Not really knowing where this conversation would be going, yet.

"So, I hear you're going to be a Lutheran teacher-preacher, or something?" She queried. "Then you must believe in God, NO?" "Ya" I chirped. "Do YOU believe that Jesus is the Son of God?" "YES!" "Do you believe in Him as your Personal Savior?" I'd never heard anyone present "it" quite like that before, Again, I smiled affirmatively, "How about the Holy Spirit of God? "Came next. "Yes, that's what all Lutherans, of all synods believe." I tersely quipped. "So I'm assuming that you then believe in **SIN** "That's where she got me right between the eyes, and then caught me in my sheepish reply.

Please remember, this took place in 1972, I was presently 21 and living in a big old house full of young male and "lightly clad" female room-mates & new visitors, by the day who did all they could, to keep enjoying many diverse legal & illegal mind adjusting type items, while they stayed with us.

SIN . . . Cere

I'm now telling you this, just because, when we moved in to that second place, we found a three lb. coffee can, full of marijuana sitting on the kitchen table, and more containers of illicit chemicals in the refrigerator than I could fathom. Believe this or not, Rick & I honestly and truly partook in nothing stronger than marijuana or occasionally some hashish. But we didn't do anything about the presence of all the rest; either. We were both too scared to say anything, because the "visitors" that came, sure didn't seem to be too cordial to us. They would play with their switch-blades and handguns, while laying around listening to the "quad-system" L.P's that we had there. "Heavy Metal" music was so popular.

Rick and I were both raised with pretty strict moral and ethical rules and conditions in our lives, and the weirdest thing (at this time) was, we never knew who we'd meet in the morning and who was at least in some form of undergarments be they male or female, the troop of guys that came through that apartment, was staggering, just in one year, and our other room-mates didn't necessarily know them either. But you, know "so & so, who knows so & so, don't you?"

Our bedroom, (Rick's & mine) was on one corner of the house (slit in window, red lights-cops?) with its own door into the bath room, and the other one was in to the kitchen. We got lots of visitors throughout the evening, looking for the "crapper" or whatever they wanted to call it. And when we got up, OH Boy, It was always an enlightening experience as to just who you might "bump" into, while trying to get to the "john"; and the girls were never friendly in the morning, when we'd stumble into them on the "twy", because nobody shut or locked the doors.

See why I was so sheepish in affirming a "yes" to her question of believing in sin? Living conditions in that place could have been the definitive point of exemplifying it.

Then she (Lois) continued, "Therefore, I'm sure you'd agree that those sins **must** be paid for, somehow if you want to go to Heaven; right? God is not expected to put up with all of that in Heaven is He?" I shook my head in a guilty negative. Then I, trying to defend myself asked, "Do you know anything about the Lutheran doctrine?" With that question I glaringly puzzled her. "Oh ya, I just want to make sure that we both agree on some of these issues and conditions. You do also believe that Jesus shed His blood and died on the cross for ALL those sins; don't you?" "YES, Of course" I quickly snapped.

"Well we can then, conclude that you know you're going to heaven; correct? When you die, RIGHT?" "I sure would like to think so, but who the heck can know something like that for sure?" I asked in a very requesting and redeeming tone. "Wow! You sure don't know your Bible, do you, pal?" That remark did get under my collar. "Look, I've been studying the Bible now since I was little, then all the way through the whole Concordia ministerial system, high-school and college/University. It seems like that's all I do."

the best way to preach . . . keep your mouth shut?

"Then You're in really "deep trouble," buster, and anyone who listens to you preach or teach is in deep trouble right along with you, if you don't even know if you're going to heaven or not." She cracked off. "Boy your somethin' else." she moaned.

"Who can know anything like that, for sure? Look, I was baptized, then confirmed. I went to Sunday school and Church, all the time, now all this {pastoral studies} thing, I went to a boys only ministerial high school, then junior college, now coming down here to River Forest, after learning Latin, German, Greek, and then just how to preach and write sermons. I even had to take a class called Hermeneutics, wouldn't that improve my odds?" I insistently queried.

"NOPE," was her instant response? "Not One Bit; You really are quite a fool, aren't you?" My immediate inner reaction (internally) was, "What Guts You've Got woman. Who do you think you are lady?" But I tensely sat there, now, very curiously Hot and definitely Bothered by how she could be so almost arrogantly crass; but I was in her house now, in her Bible-study, "rap" session. So I didn't feel that I had the right to verbally retaliate on her.

"Just what do you mean by that?" I almost demanded. She was not like this, at all, while she was teaching the class. But now, Man, did she come across like some "king/queen of conviction," or judge. She put both elbows on the table, across from me, and looked me in the eye, and stared at me; then she asked.

"How many of your sins, can you pay for, doing all that?" I shook my head back and forth & mumbled "none." "I don't care . . . No God doesn't care, what your sponsors said at your baptism. Did you then later really put all your trust in Jesus at your confirmation?" "No", I popped back. "I said what I had to say, then went through the whole procedure, and had a nice party with my parents and relatives, that's all." "No wait, I did really read and tried to learn my Luther's Small Catechism, so I would have more understanding. My mom even got me this really cool *Thomas Nelson Chain reference* study Bible, too." "So, let me see . . ." Do you really think that your pastor, or education or all those degree's will pay for so much as one of your sins?" "Of course NOT" I brashly affirmed, and quickly snapped back. "Oh doing all those sacraments like communion, will pay for your sins then hmmm?" She very brusquely quipped.

I'm 18 inches short

"Then guess what *pal,* You ARE Going to Hell! And You Are Missing Heaven by a whopping **18** inches," as she motioned from her head to her heart. So God **Must** Send You to Hell!" "What! Why? Doesn't he love Me.? I cried out. I believe in Jesus, I go to communion, I pray and I really Do Believe in God." "Grrreaat" . . . She dragged out. And which one of those actions of Yours, will pay for so much as one of your sins?" She came back with again. "Tell me something, Just who do you think you are; that **you can help God,** get you to Heaven?" "Do you really think that you can get away with putting yourself above Jesus, with your own personal actions, and achievements, to help Him pay for so much as **one** of your sins?" "NO! Of course Not!" I stammered "Then if you can't put your

Complete & TOTAL trust in what He Has "Already" done for you, you might as well be slapping God in the face. Because that's what it's like . . . See?" He died for you, as a Holy Righteous God, then took yours, mine, and everybody else's sins on Himself. He literally, Became sin Just for You! He had to pay for the damnation those sins would cause. So how can you pay for so much as **one** sin? You're telling me that you know the Bible; then good, what did Jesus say to, Nicodemus, in John 3? You know, that old Jewish Pharisee and religious ruler, in the beginning of the gospel of John 3?" "Uh . . . I don't exactly know. I "sorta" remember I humiliatingly said.

As she flung her head to the side she bewailed these words "This is just too much, you are going to be a Lutheran, preacher/teacher/ leader. And you don't know the gospel of John chapter 3? "Of course I do; John 3: 16 is one of my favorite verses." Well, how can you even graduate?" She flipped her Bible open to John chapter 3 and spun it around and poked her finger into the first verse and said to me "Here read this and tell me what it means."

isn't once enough?

I started to read out loud, quietly but just loud enough so she could still hear me, above the noise.

John 3: 1 *"The same came to Jesus by night and said unto him, Rabboni, (teacher) we know that thou are a teacher come from God, for no man can do these miracle that thou doest, except God be with him. Jesus answered and said unto him, "verily verily, I say unto thee, except a man be **born again**, he <u>cannot</u> see the kingdom of God. Nicodemus saith unto him, How can a man be born when he is old? Can he enter the second time into his mothers womb, and be born?" Jesus answered," Verily, verily I say unto thee, Except a man be born of water and of the Spirit, he <u>cannot</u> enter the kingdom of God. That which is born of the flesh is flesh; and that which is born of the Spirit is spirit."* "*Marvel not that I said unto thee, ye <u>must be born again.</u>*"

"It says *"A man,"* not a baby, but an adult, at least somebody that can understand what sin is. Infant baptism can't give salvation, when it isn't accepted by the little one. It says *"MUST,"* not here is a good alternative, or another option for you to consider. It's a **MUST BE!**"

Boy; did that hurt. She was right. I had just never looked at it clearly enough before, and that was making me feel pretty downright stupid and very unworthily guilty of anything God could do for me, at that time. She got up and just turned and smiled, and said "just think about that for a while".

I don't know if I even nodded, but she sure hit IT right on the head. I AM an IDIOT. Not to have seen this before. It is so obvious now Who do I think I am? . . . kept going through my head. If, I'm not doing it totally by Faith and faith alone; Nothing else Will Work? That makes so much sense.

As she passed by, a few minutes later, I motioned, and asked, her "What about the sins, that I commit in the future?" "Look—Dave. When Jesus died for your sins, they were ALL in the future, not just up to now. Remember that." And she moved on to talk to some others, standing by the steps.

That night around 10-10:30 I got up and left, and headed for Milwaukee, in a total quandary as to the real meaning of my life and who the heck I think I am. I am trying to show Him (God) how worthy I am; while He is trying to get me to see how unworthy, I really am. But How Much Love, He has for me anyhow. Man that is so clear Now. I shared before how I took History as a major, and I did love learning about the Greek and Roman empires.

Maybe you'll remember this too. When Caesar was warned to "Beware the Ides of March". Something traumatic was going to happen to him. Then, as we learned; Caesar's close friend and minion Brutus, stabbed and killed Caesar. Who while collapsing and dying looked at his "confidant" "Et tu Brute?" (I guess I did learn more Latin . . . it means You too Brutus?). At least the narrative was according to William Shakespeare, anyhow Guess what the Ides of March is? The fifteenth day. Guess what the Ides March 1972 was. Yup that night; very Traumatic. Keep reading, you'll see.

So as I'm driving along, going north on the Eden's expressway, late on a Wednesday night, it was pretty quiet. I had a lot of time to mull over her comments, and somewhere between northern Chicago, and southern Milwaukee, WI. I came to realize; (It takes me a while.) (hey—I "ain't the sharpest knife in the drawer-OK), that I just could Not be good enough to do **anything** for my sin, except put my full faith and trust in what Jesus had already done for me on that cross. I couldn't put any trust in my baptism, communion, education, or religious leaders. Paying penance, or giving sacrificially; NOTHING! When "It" was required that He shed His perfect pure (pre-cross, sinless) blood, to wash my sins (all of them–past present & future) AWAY! Ezekiel 18: 20 says *"The soul that sinneth, it shall die."*

I don't know if I cried out loud, or just in my mind and heart. **Thank You Jesus for saving me.!** At that very second my eternity changed from eternal damnation to eternal salvation. WOW! O.M.G! (did I get the right?)

I did know the Bible verse that says *"Without the shedding of blood, there is no forgiveness of sin."* Hebrews 9:22 A strange book to the Jews, written in the New Testament, equally for Gentiles (non-Jews), but if you think about it; it applies to everybody anyhow.

What really "dawned" on me, when she was telling me these things, which hadn't been anything easily understood by me prior, was that, when Jesus died, All my sins were future tense; not just the ones in my past. And His and only His blood was pure enough to pay that price. No religion, or act or performance was going to be able to pay for my sins, or anyone else's, either. Only What He Had Done; for me and everyone on **THAT CROSS!**

Chap. 7

Real Life

N ow you've already read about my college days, but not all the extra various activities, such as once in the summer time when three younger male adults, pulled up to our store in a big rental truck, to check out, which, at that time was a whole new concept of an ATV—or sort-of, let's say. They had six big balloon type tires, and an oval shaped body made of fiberglass that almost looked like an over-size bathtub. The one brand that we carried was called the Allis Chalmers *Terra Tiger*. Yup, it too had one of those whopping 13 hp single cylinder two stroke engines. Oh ya, we also took on Allis Chalmers lawn & garden products then too, and we even became the Wisconsin warehouse distributor for all of them.

And, so when these three mid-twenties fellas pulled up in a big utility truck. They came over to check out these *Terra Tiger's*. I eagerly and enthusiastically, as a twenty year old "big toy" salesperson, went outside to talk with them; not having any idea who they might be in that big rented box truck that they had just pulled up in.

Besides the buildings, we had almost 17 weed and grassy acres in the back of the truck/stop parking lot, and after talking with them for a while, I offered to let them go for a test-ride in it, just so they could see what it was like. After they came back gloriously "pumped" and all excited over the fun, they just had; they talked a little more with me about it, and the price. They thanked me for the "good service" and said good-bye. They then got around to asking what our selling price was. I told them they smiled and kept moving away.

Let 3 *sleeping* Dogs lie (at Night)

Then, as they were walking back to their truck, the driver turned around and asked me if I liked the big famous rock group; (at the time) *3 Dog Night*. Absolutely! Of course I joyfully hollered back. YES; Hey, Come on now, this was 1971, they were *hot,* back then. The driver walked back over to me and said. "Because, you were so extremely nice and helpful and friendly and gave us, those {demo} test rides." The driver said to me, "we'll give you four FREE tickets to come see them tomorrow night and after the show, you can come back-stage and meet the band members." I almost leapt out of my shorts with excitement and thanked them profusely.

I had never met any "Roadies" before, and I really didn't know how much "Clout" they might have. But . . . Now . . . I had one Major problem, ta *da* "who am I going to get to go with me?"

You'll notice too, that so far I haven't said so much as a word about any girlfriends, (of mine) or my love life in general. I did have a few buddies, that I could call to invite, but I already knew they weren't going to be available, tomorrow night. There was a young lady, who lived on the other side of my parent's lake, whose daddy was (get this—the police chief of the little city that oversaw the lake, as well. I got along great with her whole family and helped keep things working like, lawn mowers, and sump pumps, in the basement, etc. And I never got stopped with my little "econo" car, either. (Just wait)

Yup, I decided to call my classmate friend, and room-mate (remember) Rick, who was living with his mom & dad for the summer, too. They lived way out in a suburb northwest of Milwaukee, while I lived way out in the south-west of the city. We didn't see each other during the summer. So I called him and I knew that he was seeing that girl from Milwaukee, remember, she was going to college down in River Forest too, where we were going, as well. He said sure, he would like to go, and would check with his girlfriend, Jen, if she could make it, and wanted to come, too.

Oh . . . NO! Now Who?

Then came the dreaded question . . . "Who else are you going to take?" Ouch! I knew that was coming, and I didn't really have an answer for any one that I'd care to ask, and it was now summer, & we both were out of the Concordia Milwaukee scene, and being the summer break anyhow there was no one around.

Rick, then reminded me that Jen. had a sister who was a couple of years younger, who might be interested in "just coming along" with us, if I still had that one ticket left. Can we say **Blind Date!** You've got to admit, _if_ it had to be a blind date, this couldn't have been much better. A *3 Dog Night concert* and free tickets-backstage passes. So I thought, I sure hope that this was going to be a "good time" if she agrees, that is. Several hours later, my heart was pounding with anticipation for a 1. a date, 2. to see *3 Dog Night* up front, 3. and it should be close to free!

You see back then I was earning a huge $1.85 an hour. So you might think I was flush with cash, right? (Suurrre). There was one expense that I hadn't really covered yet, and that was the now (my) new/used car that I had just gotten with only around 2000 miles on it. Remember the Nova economy car that I mentioned earlier, when we got back to school in Illinois, I would so enjoy driving that "baby" back and forth, (for a while any way) you'll see. I had previously bought my mom's now old six cylinder automatic, '61 Chevy Impala, (that couldn't get out of its own way) and drove that till I found this "nice little "econo" car. (just wait) Remember, I told you we were "frugal" and quite conservative. Well, I put my sales training talents (that I didn't even know I had, yet) to work and I convinced my parents that IT was Sooo . . . economical . . . WELL Not quite; but it was a little Chevy *NOVA*!

Guys, you'll love this part. My nice little economy car just so happened to be, a quite rare 1969 Chevy Nova. Oh ya, did I fail to mention that it was a factory built, and dealer rebuilt (for acceleration) SS **396** Nova. There were only 500 ever made by GM. They made 500 Camaro's, and 500 Nova's, with 396 cubic inch motors; after that they all went to 350 ci. A 4-speed Hurst, power shifter and a very "finicky" double barrel Holley carburetor, and it had a **"killer"** clutch like you can't imagine just how hard that thing was to push down. (More on that part . . . soon)

Back to the *3 Dog Night* dilemma, that I was confronted with. A few hours later Rick called and told me that his girlfriend's sister would be interested in coming with us. So the "Date was On!" Yaaa. He and I met by the old Concordia campus (Milwaukee) near the mid part of the city, and then drove a little ways north, in town to pick up the two sisters. In today's jargon they were both really "hot", and her (Jen's) sister was absolutely gorgeous, (today "smokin" hot) she had long straight medium brown hair, or maybe straight medium blonde (it had become my first real date in a long time) and she had a perfect figure, wow! "There truly is a Heaven!" I thought as I opened the door and pulled the seat forward for Rick and Jen. to get in the backseat. So her sister and I could be "oh so" comfortable in the front seat, NO? . . . As she got in and we were headed for downtown. I had so sadly forgotten; but I told you that it had a four speed *Hurst* shifter. RIGHT IN The Middle of the two, front seats. Great!

"Clutching" for a date

We came into the back of the arena, and showed our passes to the guard, and he let us walk right in; and escorted us right to the front row center seats. 3-4 for feet away from this very popular group. It was fantastic, when one of the "roadies" came out after the show and escorted us in under the stage and introduced us to all the band members individually. Oh So Cool! That was truly a great way to start a first date. But, Then came the real fun (facetiously said; you'll" see). We walked a few blocks, back to the car which was parked in a multilayer parking structure. We were on the very bottom level, with a ton of cars leaving just when we were, of course.

Now, guys; this is where you're going to "grunt with laughter. But only if you have ever had or drove a sort of "muscle car" with a super-strong manual clutch. After talking all the while of how great our experience had just been. We all hopped into "my new" high performance muscle car, and finally got a chance to back out of the stall because there were so many cars, then we started our long–long wait in line to go up the three separate ramps to pay the teller and then get out. OUCH! YA, It started already, No no, not the necking or anything, but my super *stiff* (ya, which I was still trying to get used to), heavy duty, **clutch lever,** guys. Sitting on the level, literally creeping a foot or two at a time, was bad enough, just trying to keep that Holley carb. working at idle; but when we hit the first ramp and I had to keep my left foot on the clutch—in first gear, and my right foot on the brake so I wouldn't roll backwards into the car that (was very close) behind me, things in my life got real tense all around; due to the clutch and that **Big** four barrel *Holley* carb. Please fellas, "cut me some slack" I had only driven this car for a couple of weeks, now. So I wasn't really used to it that much, yet.

Left leg—**Muscle Car?**

By the second ramp up, my left leg was in so much pain. I was afraid it might go numb. I just wanted to jump out and scream, but what do I do? The car actually stalled out on me a couple of times, and I wasn't smooth enough, to keep it running. With my right foot, I had to slip back and forth, between the brakes and throttle, that didn't go too well, and that didn't mean I'd get it running right away either. It was a major trick for me to do that, let's just say. The short bit of level surface, between ramps, offered very little relief. When I finally got to the top of the incline. That's for sure, and it didn't seem to last too long either, and "here we go again."

I thought to myself, this is pure agony, I hope it's going to be worth it all. Ya know . . . The other three just sat there seeing the extreme pain I was in by the expressions on my face as I grit my teeth, from all the torture that I was in, but at least they didn't snicker or laugh. (too hard)

Everybody in the car knew that I was having a great deal of difficulty, especially when we would start rolling backwards, into the car behind us, because I was trying to keep the engine running,(Ala *Holley* four barrel-thank you) and then it stalled on me twice and I couldn't 1. give it gas, 2. hold the brake down, to keep from sliding backwards 3.hold the clutch in just right, to keep it from stalling or lurching (by now, it Hurt so Bad), 4. get the engine started again. What parking brake? Oh ya that little pedal down on the left. "Alright, so I forgot it. Duh, and I hadn't ever even used it yet.

This first date was turning into a real painful adventure, at least for me {3 Dog night<u>mare</u>} (cute-huh?) FINALLY we got to the top level and crept towards the check-out stand, and I was ready to cry. I was in so much leg pain. But we still went to a local diner called "Big Boy" and had a little bit to eat, and I couldn't tell them about all of my painful woes, because the girls would have seen me as such a "wuss", even though I walked in with such a goofy limp, in my leg, It was so stiff after all that; in my left leg, and whole upper-groin area. Things seemed to end pretty well all-in-all (friendly) that night, and we got the girls home and went back to Rick's car.

Look Out <u>Providence</u>; Here we come Again

Yes it's true, Rick and I eventually did become brother-in-laws. Yup, yes we did. We married a sister. Two beautiful women, who shared like values, and "mores." It sure kept the "in-laws" in check.

A few weeks later, when we got back to Chicago, I moved all of what little belongings I had, back to Milwaukee (in my economy car) and worked at the cycle shop. And so I squeezed hard on Hank that was, to now let me leave a little early just on Wednesdays, & that was "killing" him to let me go; mainly because I was really the only sales person that we had there. The real "fun" part about that job (ha ha) was that we were open from 9 am–9 pm Monday thru Friday, and then from 9–6 on Saturday. So now, do you still really wonder, why I haven't talked about girls before this? Hmm . . . When Hank did talk in his "old world" manor and his sort of "charm," he would BARK at the customers almost demanding that they better buy something, because he told them to. And that really didn't go over so well with a lot of customers! (even back then–no really)

You've gotta realize that I was just waiting for the religious "call" but "It", was real-quiet, on the recruitment side of things at that time. So I started going back down into Chicago, on Wednesday nights, and I invited a few others, some were friend or customers, and even just some other acquaintances, to join me. Because I just worked at the cycle shop and started saving my pennies, as best I could, we would car pool and "chip" in for gas, or else take our bikes. (Kawasaki of course—that is)

My now "old" college room-mate Rick and Jen, would usually also come along, and sure enough so did her sister. (nice huh?) I sometimes drove, but I couldn't really do it a lot, because the "Jimmy Carter" oil embargo took place and kicked in to our (Hank's) gas stations, and we would all have to sit in lines waiting for gas. Well, I could sit, I just couldn't afford to buy much gas any more. Here is why. Don't laugh, and don't think I'm lying; but at the cycle shop, Hank, the truck-stop/gas station owner, before the embargo kicked in; his Cities Service gas station was selling regular for (YES) for just 19 cents a gallon, then in a little over a month it had "sky-rocketed to 49 cents a gallon, and in those days, that financially almost "ate me alive" in my nice little "**econo**" car. With that Holley, I could get a whopping 8 miles per gallon. (that really did hurt-a lot). I never once got better than those 8 miles per, and it would have to be filled up after just one run to Chicago. (Each way!) As you can bet, I drove my "demo" bike, a lot. Thank You, Kawasaki for the great gas mileage!

But what made up for those costs, that I had incurred, was through some pretty outstanding sales numbers, an absolutely incredible opportunity was given to me, to get to go on {very lavish} free trips starting with one in the late summer of 1971. I was given the chance to go on an "all-expense paid" top-shelf" trip, by Kawasaki; to Japan. To get to go sight see, and visit the motorcycle manufacturing plant, down in Akashi. That is where you want to speak about quality, the line production assembly people, all wore white gloves (and they stayed that way while working). That in itself started to impress me about their quality.

We were introduced to the brand new "monster" H2 750 triple, two stroke. Three cylinder cycle. At that plant they even had their own nice big oval race track with canted corners and everything; right on the grounds and we even got to watch them and sit right up front as they were demonstrating it for us on sometimes just one but usually two wheels. WOW, Was it fast! Things like that, and many more, was what got me motivated to really sell a lot more Kawasaki's and they knew it, that's why they showed off their facilities and wares. I was truly becoming very enamored with them.

They also; while we were over there, took us to Hong Kong, China. Which, back then was still under the United Kingdom's control (England—for you history scholars) and Taipei Taiwan. I just loved learning about the different cultures, first hand. The differences in peoples in their cultures, and character and even their architecture was so very outstanding and educational for me.

After graduation, remember ours was that tri-mester thing, we finished in mid-March, I just stayed busy at the store, and in my spare time at home, I would go into the basement and try my best at electronics, by building a "Heath kit" stereo receiver, it was a difficult and elaborate kit, but I soon learned how to solder, and learn what a diode, and a capacitor was. When my parents weren't in the house I would practice on my beautiful Ludwig drum set, too. But otherwise life for me was pretty "humdrum", because financially, like I said, there weren't many other options. But remember I was still living at the lake, so I did get to fish a lot, and swim, but most of all, we got to bring a Jet Ski out and I spent a lot of time riding that on beautiful Lake Denoon. It was so much fun. I just loved it to pieces.

Missionary Journey to Marriage

Except that, I had been going out with Jen's, sister now. A real, live, girlfriend; whom I was starting to get very attracted to, she seemed to like me, wonder of all wonders too. To this day, although I have no idea why.

After a really "long time "dating that is; that spring and summer, (about 3 months or so) I broke down and proposed to her. Now what is really interesting, is that it's just not how I do things, quickly like that spontaneous, or emotional. I'm the kind of person that likes to really study "things" our first, and understand as many variables, scenarios and conditions as possible, so why am I doing this? You'll see later, why I'm bringing this up. I couldn't understand myself, it was just so unnatural for me, but I knew I was going to do it. And I had no "clear headed" understanding as to why (not that!), and why right now? Was I afraid of losing this "really hot chick? No. She was the only one who would accept me. I hope not. Then why so quick? I didn't know, myself.

Remember I introduced you to Mr. Guts(y), well one evening after we went for a ride and had something to eat, (remember, I was poor), I pulled up across from her parents' house, and we were listening to the radio, and I simply turned to her and told her how much she meant to me and I was just wondering if she would be interested in marrying me. Now this gal is so quiet, I didn't have any idea, what she might say, and I really didn't even expect an answer yet, especially after only having met me and gone out for a few months . . . "WHAT AM I DOING?"

And then what will she do? I wasn't sure that I really wanted her to say YES, but as "they say" guts I do have, I guess. Is that because

I'm a lefty or an only child, or just plain courageous, or maybe just crazy or stupid. Who knows, I thought, so here goes.

Maybe that means I don't get "scared too easily." But I sure was that night in the car. Thinking that there would be {a long pause that would let me know just how she really felt} she quickly came back with "YES." I certainly was committed; NOW. And I sure wasn't expecting that either, but I then (like I often do) started to qualify this whole thing; by saying I'll only marry you if you believe like I do, that this means "for life." Then came the smiling nod of agreement, with a faint little "ya". Good . . . "And don't marry me for money, 'cuz I probably won't have much". Another positive nod. "Look; and I sure don't have a lot of money now, either, but I am working, and someday the whole motorcycle thing is supposed to be mine, {so I'm told,} but let's not count on that; OK?" Now looking back; that was really smart one my part, to tell her that then, times could get real lean, as you'll see if there is another book.

Yes it's true, Rick and I eventually did become brother-in-laws. Yup, Yes we did. We married a sister. Two beautiful women, who shared like values, and "mores." It sure kept the "in-laws" in check.

As we then began to prepare for our future, we talked it over and both agreed that we wanted to become missionaries, possibly to New Guinea, so we got a lot of different folk's impressions, and they all said "If you can handle all the sacrifice then go for it". So we applied to *New Tribes Bible Institute,* which had its main school about 20 minutes from my parent's house, in Waukesha, WI. We thought that we would go there for the first 3 years of training, and then off to one of the two "boot camps" (designed to prepare you to live in the jungle) and then back down to Missouri, where they had a language school.

This life activity appealed to both of us, and we were totally ready to head off in, 3 or 4 months after we got married in late May of that following year. Then as seen by me often in life, there was a "big "surprise, thrown into the mix, again. New Tribes sent us a letter of acceptance and told us to be at the school by mid-August, just to be at the one now 300 miles away, in Michigan. Because, instead of them enrolling us in the school 20 minutes from my existing home; where I could still drive off to work at the cycle shop, in the afternoons, so we could survive the tuition and cost of living; they told us that our school was going to be at a brand new facility that was just being prepared in Jackson Michigan, and we were going to be one of their very first students on that campus. Which consisted of <u>one</u> little old hotel building in the middle of the old downtown Jackson. GREattt . . . !

Change—"the most constant"

So now everything was about to change, in our plans again. Well, when our parents heard about us becoming missionaries, you can guess what hit the fan. And it *hit* hard, really, really hard. But we both were committed to following through with it, because the people that we had met over the last several months, and now years, for me now, was almost unbelievably enlightening. These folks were not "in it" for the money, or fame, glory, or power, just for a strong heart felt gratitude for the gift that they had been so freely given.

As you saw earlier, my ministerial training in high-school and college, showed me one side of "mainstream liturgical church." I really didn't care for much of that kind of church, and that was, as we were ending our tenure as students, they were trying to get us as prepared as they could to withstand challenges and obstacles for our future in the ministry, of say at a church or school. The point was just to learn how to deal with the "politics", and I don't want to say "manipulate," but rather "deeply influence congregations and various church groups. Here, I have to confess, that really turned me "off." And got me to start searching for more truth, not politics or games.

I'm not implying that the priest, rabbi or pastor or your church or synagogue, or even an Imam in your temple, has these intentions, foremost in their mind. Just to keep a congregation and the offerings coming, there has to be a type of "bait and hook" mentality, (this is a fact that we learned in business training). I didn't say "bait and switch" like retail companies are famous for, but rather as you may even recognize in your own religious background, (if you are in any religion). Too often "guilt, shame, obligation, unworthiness, or desperate ability" are devises used to attain, is strongly emphasized to continue to have the congregants keep attending. And that their purses and wallets, need to remain "open" as well. (yuk)

Later I realized that the Lutheran training spent the greatest amount of time on the 4 Gospels (Matthew, Mark, Luke, John) and very little emphasis on the Epistles (letters) like Romans, Galatians, Philippians, Colossian's, etc. And they would not "touch" the book of Revelation with a ten foot pole. Even though Martin Luther (he was Awesome) loved the book of Romans so much.

Then too, the whole "missionary thing" really appealed to me, I wanted to serve God, not bureaucracy, and committees, and then have to play "mind games." I sure didn't see that as very "spiritual" at all. (Okay all you religious leaders that are reading this; go ahead just blame Me or maybe Kawasaki for those comments.) Only if you really disagree. Hmm.

Now I just have to tell you a quick really "good one "One of our customer, whose name was Tom. He was a senior in high-school at the time, had bought one of those crazy hot Kawasaki H2 750 triples. My wife, Elsbeth and I, kind of made friends with him, and he would come over to our little apartment, just to get something to eat, and whiles there, he would unload all of his life's issues about school, home, girlfriends and anything else that bothered him, on us. We became his "sounding boards", at the time. He got so comfortable with us and saw that we were concerned more with his well-being, that we invited him down to the Chicago Bible-study (rap session) Soon he began to really see a much greater value in life, and To His Own Personal life, and so he began to "mellow-out" and used our place as a type of little sanctuary of peace and calm being so different to the other parts of his life.

My wife and I were definitely hoping that he would come to personally know God, on his own, because otherwise he was headed for some real "deep" serious problems in life, which we knew were only going to lead to his destruction. We were becoming pretty close as friends, and he had so much "enthusiasm" overall, it was just fun to be with him. (you'll see)

This is the part that was just so funny (kids–don't do this at home). He and I would go for motorcycle rides, down some nice big busy streets in Milwaukee. And when the time was "just right", like when two kids would be walking down the sidewalk, just ahead of us. He would come up from behind them and "rev" the heck out of that noisy bike and he would accelerate behind them and just when he got up next to them on the road, he'd scream and slam on the brakes and rev the motor more, with the tires squealing, loudly. One time we saw one teenager, who was closer to the road, literally throw himself into the arms of his buddy on the sidewalk, in total fear. There were a few little old folks getting on a bus that got their blood pressure up, as well. Shame *Shame Shame*. We were really naughty; hey? But you "gotta know" he's the one who I recognized in the hospital, when he'd come up to see me, while still unconscious. He' So Great! Get this; he can even make the unconscious laugh. We couldn't laugh harder, when we were riding, than we did. (innocent fun?)

As I was saying earlier; upon finding out about our decision to be missionaries, our parents all decided to not supply any help in our marriage plans. This put a real stretch on our time and finances. But still we were able to gather support from all levels of friends. We got married in a mid-town Bible church and held the "whole thing" right there. The grandma lady Lois, from the {rap session} in Chicago, whose house we went down to, her husband Don and family catered the food for us right in that church basement. All went well. Another interesting tid-bit to note, is as of this writing, we've now been married, (only) 40 years. (Sorry Honey)

Love of My Life *almost* gone?

But now, my true genuine and real heart's love is, at this point now my new beautiful bride. (No not Kawasaki) And then to come in a few years, would be our children, our two boys. But there was some real challenging moments in all of that, as well, you'll see.

One weekend morning in early spring of '74, **after** we had gotten back from Michigan, my wife, Elsbeth, (the early riser) unlike herself, stayed, lying in bed and started to utter groans under her breath, and told me she wasn't able to move and she couldn't even get up and out of bed. She was experiencing so much stomach pain. Now, what do I do? I called my mom, who (remember) worked for that doctor, I told you about earlier. He was a G.P. (general Practitioner) and a surgical Doctor as well. She called him, and he insisted that we go to the hospital, that he works from, about 20 miles to the west. Ya and get this. It was only about 15 blocks from the other New Tribes Mission School that we thought we were going to attend. (ha-ha). Ironically, we were less than 1 mile away from the major trauma hospital, where years later, I spent a lot of time, we headed out. Nervously, I gave it my all and gently lifted and carried Elsbeth to the car. She was in such extreme pain, that I was on the verge of panic.

We sped off to the hospital, and in about 20 minutes we got to the emergency entrance, they brought out a gurney, (stretcher) and lifted her right in. When we got up to an examining room they made me stay out in the hall. I sat there in such a sweat, and after a few minutes a young man came walking briskly down the hall, with the absolutely longest hypodermic needle I had ever seen or even imagined. It looked to be at least 18" or maybe more. He opened the door to the room my wife was in and I leapt up to yank it out of his hand, I sure startled the "liven heck" out of him. He just said he was following orders. I swore that they better not plan on using that on my wife, and he just shrugged me off.

"They really weren't going to use that on my wife" I hoped and prayed. Then I heard some long loud screams, but the door was locked, and I couldn't get in. Probably a good thing all in all. Then about a half hour went by when a nurse came out and told me that they were taking her surgery immediately, as in "Right Now!" She was having a tubular pregnancy. This was very serious, because she had lost so much blood, already, that it was just "floating" in her abdomen.

I was so scared. Added to all I could do was wait by myself. This, remember was way before cell phones, and up where I was I couldn't see any telephone to call my parents, or anyone else. After several hours they let me go in to her recovery room, and sit there as she laid under anesthesia. When she finally came too, she was real *real weak,* and they told me not to cause any commotion, for her. It seemed like forever, but they finally let her go home after a few days. However nobody would tell me what was going on, in there.

A few weeks later, I asked my mom. She told me that the doctor, who she worked for, said that my wife had lost over 3 1/2 pints of blood, and that her tube had burst and her abdomen was full of all those pints of now useless blood . . . He also told her that my wife had been given a 50/50 chance of survival through it all. Some more trauma to my life; and hers. Then after she healed up, she went back to work, at the motorcycle shop with me, as our receptionist and for a while, our life was then going pretty smooth again.

A couple of years later, my wife let me know that she was pregnant again. And we got all excited, and this anticipation lasted for six months, when she cried out in pain, one more time, and I got her to the hospital once more, and this time she had suffered a miscarriage. It was a little girl, like we were both kind-of hoping for. It happened on September 13th of 1976. She again stayed home and recouped back to health quite well, and we were just praying that it wouldn't be the end of our being parents.

The *Third* First

That next February, Elsbeth once again announced to me, her pregnancy, and that she should probably be due in late fall around mid to late October. So again with excitement we prayed all would go well for her and the baby. She was working at the cycle shop yet, before she just couldn't any more. Then one day in early to mid Sept. she got really bad aches and pains in her abdomen, so we took her to the doctor (pediatrician) and they told us to get right to the hospital.

That day, Yes! September 13th 1977, exactly ONE year later, to the day she gave birth to a beautiful baby (good thing—huh) boy. He and mom were both good and healthy. We had the girls names all picked out, but we just couldn't agree on a boy's name, 'till suddenly one of us said "Eric, and we both agreed. And so it was our first son, Eric David Miles. We were very happy and rejoiced in this new little miracle. Can you believe that or what . . . same day, and over a month early?

Now maybe you'll be able to forgive him, if he has a real strong fetish for Kawasaki too. It was already in mom and dad's blood; I guess. He could ride his Kawasaki electric three wheeler before he could walk. His little toe Juussst touched the pedal. (Let the Good Times Roll)

Chap. 8

Back to School

Now, let's back up a bit right here. Back tracking to mid-August of 1973, we've been married a whole 2 ½ months, so these "old timers" boxed up everything we had (which sure wasn't much) and went from Milwaukee, to Jackson Michigan. This young fella Tom, our new friend and helper, offered to help load the truck and then even go along with us to get moved in to the new school. He put his motorcycle in the back of the truck that still had plenty of extra room; remember I said, we sure didn't have a lot of home goods and furniture.

So we drove through Chicago, and half way through Michigan, until we got to Jackson, and found this nice little old 4 story hotel in the middle of this old established city and, we pulled up to the door and checked in and started unloading. Up to that point, I had still been smoking, not a lot (half a pack a day-maybe), but New Tribes School policy was that there was NO SMOKING! At all for students or staff alike. I finished my last cigarette, in the pack, right down to the filter. And crushed it out on the front door step, and said to myself, how can I be under the control of a stupid little piece of paper and tobacco, and still say that I'm giving myself to Jesus and submit myself to him. So that was the Last One, for me. (cigarette-no-honest)

If only you could have been there, that day we got all moved in. My wife started to re-arrange and put whatever we could "away."

Tom and I checked out the "campus" ha ha, all three floors (we had access to) of the one building. I was so glad when some of the other guys that were staying on a floor above us, "kinda" took Tom "in" as a friend, and invited him up to their rooms, and we never saw him AGAIN!, until the next morning that is. We instantly recognized him at the cafeteria breakfast, but he "definitely" Was Not the same person we saw go up those stairs the night before. WOW! What a transition.

He was a "whole new" person "literally," language, demeanor, attitude, down-right to the way he carried himself. Something sure happened up their last night, was what we both thought and were so hopeful for.

Our apartment, (really little living quarters) was a big and spacious (NOT) two rooms (like an efficiency) with a sink and stove, and the newest decor was a big pile of bricks in the middle of the kitchen/living-room floor. It was about three feet by three feet, by four feet high. When I inquired, they said that they needed to keep the bricks there, because there was no room in the hall way or anywhere else, and we would just have to live around it this school year, they need them to fix the chimney.

Hold the Ropes

There was NO bathroom in the rooms, just a "joint" one down the hall. We all had to check to see who was in there. (always interesting) Oh Boy! We really both liked the school (not the building) and its classes on different books of the Bible. There was one time period every day that was called "Hold the Ropes." It wasn't an actual class, rather a time to listen to somebody read reports from different missionaries that were stationed all over the globe. Their successes, their trials, their fears, their incidents of brutality by the different tribes of peoples. If you didn't come away every day, in tears, either of joy or sorrow, you just didn't have a heart. It was so powerful and moving, and it so "proved" God and His existence over and over again.

We would hear of missionaries say in Papua New Guinea, and Argentina, or Brazil, even in Venezuela, or Mexico. These stories were certainly NOT made up, but were they ever powerful. And to learn how some cultures of villagers in different parts of the South Sea Islands, didn't so much as have a word of any form of "thanks" in their dialect or language. How do you approach a person with the Love of God, given to mankind and offered to all; with the simple procedure of accepting it by faith, and then try to get them to "thank Him for His Mercy?" They don't know how to thank. {If I did something for you—You just simply "owe me" now; or vise-verse}.

Now I had come from a lot of Bible training, as you've read, yet I still didn't understand clearly, right off; with memorization, and deep study; all of the concepts they were teaching. I even had to take a class on Hermeneutics again, there (cute-huh?).

Believe it or not that's not a dirty word either, it just means "Deep study of ancient literature" obviously to most of which compiled and known is the Bible. Please be aware that the Bible is Not a book. It simply is a compilation of various books assembled in 312-325 A.D. at a place called Nicaea. There were smaller compilations begun much earlier, but this brought together what we would know to be called the "King James" version, of 1611. Other Ancient literature, and some of the books of Nebuchadnezzar (you wonder what his mother had against him; to name him that, whew) we had to study out a lot of those type writing too. So, at the New Tribes School, I did listen intently and the professors were much excogitated in their studies. What I really enjoyed, was how they put a lot of scripture into a current day personal life motif that made it so much easier to visualize and understand.

Look; If you can explain {God} to somebody in a "grass skirt, with a spear in his hand, you are going to have to learn how to bring that whole thing across, very well. They (the New Tribes missionaries) are awesome at that.

Are you the kind of person, who questions the "validity" of the Bible? Maybe this will help, it took the span of over a thousand years, and a group of 40-43 different authors, and they wrote 39 Old & 27 New Testament books. They all have the same premise, (agenda let's say) and theme, They DO NOT dispute each other, if properly read in context. Have you ever played "telephone?" Where a group of people, or kids, gets together, one person is given a little phrase or maybe just a word. Then they whisper it into the ear of the person next to them, who turns and whispers what they "were sure" they just heard to the person to their other side, and around the room it goes. By the time it comes all the way around to the first person again, it usually isn't even close. So HOW all these authors in that time span of almost a millennium could keep it even close; if it wasn't God ordained? (Providence?) Just tuck that into the back of your mind.

Can You Handle This?

Please bear with me while I go "deep" for a bit, so if it is "too much" for you, just go a few paragraphs down, a little further, and the interesting "fun" will start again.

In the mission school curriculum, there was, one class that made me almost want to *crawl*. The more that this one particular professor expounded on it, as he saw Christianity to be, was very contrary to the simple gospel message, that I had now embraced, which said that your sins are paid for, completely by the death of Jesus Christ on the Cross. *"The soul that sinneth, it shall die."* Ezekiel 18:20 When He said "It is Finished" that's exactly what He meant. Total Forgiveness—Complete. When the Bible then proclaims "your sins and Iniquities will I remember No More." Hebrews 8:12. I took God at His word. And that was, as I had come to clearly learn, I'm CLEAN! But that seems to be a Biblical concept that is NOT "accepted" by so many Christians of all respects. Where the One, Yes just One, Bible verse, that so many "cling to, out of guilty desperation is" I John 1: 9 &10 *"If we confess our sins, He is faithful and just to forgive us our sins. And to cleanse us from All unrighteousness"* Does that sound like somebody who has already been cleansed; whose sins have been forgiven? I don't think so.

Just for your knowledge; one of the co-founders of the mission school, was also a pastor at a nice big church near downtown Chicago, and founder of a children's bible club. He and his wife, just so happened to be the ones to explain the clear true meaning of the Bible to this missionary lady (Lois) and her husband, back in the late forty's. His name was Dr. Lance Latham. I knew him personally, as well, and if there was a man who could just "overwhelm" you with wisdom, it sure was Doc. Latham

what if I don't have time to "confess?"

Now the professor, who was a "new" (part-time) faculty staff member from a local (very, very, fundamental type church, (please recall that this was the school's first full year of classes–in Michigan) was insisting that each and every morning during our prayer and meditation time, before classes; we must as "good little" Christians write down each and every sin that we had committed the day before, and if we had missed any prior, to include them as well. Then we were to pray I John1:9 over each sin, so we could go on our day in "righteous fellowship" with God.

I had a real problem with this. I asked myself, God, and the professors. Which sins needed "more forgiveness?" Didn't Jesus die for them ALL? How could a verse in the Book of Romans, say in chapter 5:8, *"While we were Yet sinners, Christ Died for Us."* So then what are we now? In God's eyes, were not sinners any more, but Holy Righteous children of God, else if we have any unforgiven sin, He certainly can't/won't be able to take us to Heaven. Our sins are **Paid For In Full!** Doesn't forgiven mean just that, {Forgiven?} Hebrews also tells us that Christ died for sins ONCE! So how do we pull more forgiveness out of "thin air?" The DEBT WAS PAID! And without the shedding of blood, there is NO forgiveness.

Which is the message that was echoed from the basement in Chicago, over and over. And the verse in Hebrews chapter 9:22 *". . . and without the shedding of blood there is NO Forgiveness"*. Only the Catholics and Episcopalians believe in having to re-crucify Jesus over and over again in their masses. Hebrews also says that *"He died Once unto sin."* If I pray I John 1:9, for more forgiveness, where's the blood-shedding?

Missouri Synod Lutherans are really quite conservative and with Wisconsin Synod, they "stick by the book"; in other words; the Bible even closer. They have their sacraments like infant baptism, and communion, and they stick quite close to the church calendar. But this whole teaching from this "overly guilt ridden" pastor was going off in the direction of Roman Catholicism, of pure "works righteousness" with the whole confession thing. He just couldn't accept complete redemption, and forgiveness, by Christ-alone.

Ya Ya; I know it was some pretty "heavy religious talk, but this is what has all the power to make the rest of my words become totally significant, as to what really happens after *Your* Last Breath. So please let me explain myself. I have done what seems to be almost endless hours of study, in the Bible, since my "conversion-awakening-enlightenment, or born again experience, being saved." (These are all biblical names of the same event that happens to the person who, chooses to make a personal commitment to receive Jesus Christ as their one-on-one Savior. They are used in various translations, in English and even in the Greek. And I used many other reference books, like concordances, to see if I've got this understanding absolutely accurate and correct. Because if something isn't true I Don't want to be "duped" into believing it. No! No. I'm not trying to make up any new religion or anything else. There are a lot of churches and people who know, believe and teach all this already. Many bible churches, some Baptist churches and others. This isn't anything new. Even the Roman Catholic's for hundreds and hundreds of years, sent missionaries out all over the world to proclaim Jesus to "all the nations." Man you've got to give them credit for all that effort.

And after all the reading and research I have found out that even Martin Luther, himself found true salvation by his understanding of the book of Romans Chapter 3: 23. It is what the Apostle Paul is insisting on, in almost all of his epistles. The only problem is we, folks live on such a different "plain-standard" than what God is providing for us. And we use the human idea, that we must "help God" get us to heaven, because we have to <u>DO</u> something. Which is <u>TOTALLY Wrong</u>! We just Can't do Anything, but thank and appreciate Him for, <u>He Has Done It ALL</u>! For US. Already! It is the easiest and yet the hardest thing to do . . . Trust HIM by **Faith Alone**!

God Has Done *It* & Done *It* All; and All By Himself, we can't even claim the right to believing it; just so we don't go "over the edge" with arrogance as to how smart we were to get saved. But a thankful humility to serve Him and his ordinances to the best of our ability. And NOT out of obligation.

What God wants from us, Is Not <u>just</u> obedience. What He is really looking for is our Thankfulness and Praise. If you are reading this, as a Jewish person or a "Gentile" (bible talk); I am sure you can all remember what it says in the book of Psalms 95: 2 *"Come before His presence with <u>thanksgiving</u>"* Not fear of being unaccepted or punished; we just don't realize that there is NO form of "works righteousness that God can or will accept from us in the payment of a sin. He has already <u>Done It All!</u> Thank Him for it and move on. We Need to be Faithful! After all, John 3: 16 says he died for the sins of the world. He knew us and what we are like, beforehand. And He still sacrificed Himself for Us-No-FOR-<u>You</u>!

Did you know that there will <u>Not</u> be, so much as <u>One</u> "Sinner" in Hell? (got you attention didn't I?) It is absolutely True. John 3: 16 again *"For God so loved the world that He gave His Only Begotten Son, that whosoever believes will NOT perish, but have everlasting life."* Everybody's sins have been Paid for, but only those that reach out by faith (believe) are saved. Sinners go to Hell, True Believers go to

Heaven! We are clearly told in God's Bible that we are NOT saved by good works, but <u>unto</u> good works. Ephesians 2: 10

Why Me LORD?

Many people that I know and that just know me; have tried to convince me that this is why my initial death experience likely took place. Please realize that out of everyone that I know I certainly <u>Don't</u> deserve this kind of recognition that this whole incident has brought about. I'm just a plain old motorcycle salesman, who happens to firmly believe in God and His Son Jesus Christ. And the Holy Spirit; who had Mercy on Me (especially undeserved, as I am). But because of the "revelation" that I had been gifted to learn about, being this concept of {genuine heartfelt thanksgiving}; I believe there were "other parties" involved in challenging my ability to be thankful in <u>EVERYTHING</u>! This next verse that I would like to share with you, is found in the New Testament book of I Thessalonians 5:18. *"In <u>everything</u> give thanks." Everything* is a really big word, especially when you're laying in a hospital bed, pretty much in pieces and with <u>No</u> idea what could lie ahead, for you.

Honestly, even you have to question the likely hood of being the (1) rear-ended, & only one person {me, in the middle of a hectic and busy, warm sunny Tuesday afternoon, by a "dead drunk" driver, who had just recently been out of work. The odds . . . ?

If this view of forgiveness, isn't correct, then I have even More to be thankful for. Let me explain: Seeing or not seeing the car, "rushing" up behind me (I don't remember) but even upon impact, I'm sure that I would have realized something was up (ME!) I'm not saying, I did or I didn't verbalize some less than "nice" words, or had a real bad attitude over what was just happening to me now. So if what I just said in those last paragraphs about "complete-forgiveness" isn't absolutely correct. Then if I would have "stayed dead" and stood before the "All-Mighty", in Heaven. He could have looked at me and said Sorry Dave, but you didn't confess those sinful thought and words, just now. I can't let You In. What? The escalator to Hell-You Go. Not even a Bible believer would "buy" that. That would be pretty despicable, of any "so-called" loving and merciful God, wouldn't it? No, That isn't Him (the God of the Bible); because He paid for every one of those sins ALREADY! And I believed IT!

Please read in a Torah, Bible, or even off the internet the Old Testament book of Job {'Iyyov Shirr Ha-Shari}. He was a "pawn" stuck in the middle of a spiritual challenge, and it took some horrendous tolls on him, his family, and his whole life. Maybe I'm just feeling that way, by what all happened to me, but I have to tell you that, what has become of my life since, is truly "miraculous," in itself. Amen to Job.

And guess what I found out; it is that, this is nothing new to any biblical following religion or faith. NO it's Not! We just somehow want to feel some "obligation, or conviction, or maybe fearful, not to have to "do something" "our part", or offer something. WE can't! All we can do is Accept it all!! Really . . . That's It. Ephesians (New Testament epistle) 2: 8&9 *"For by grace are saved through faith and that not of yourselves, it is the gift of God: Not of works, lest any man should boast."* That Needs No explanation or interpretation.

Even the "Great—Dr. Charles Stanley," wrote a book, that I had found a few years later; where he expounds on his "new revelation" and findings that explain forgiveness and its completeness, with God, through Jesus sacrifice. He had it "right on;" for everyone.

I certainly never had any intention of walking away from the Missouri Synod Lutheran Church, but when I saw the clarity of God's Word, and it made such obvious sense, I did move in that direction. So I'm not "stuck" in a religious position, just to be there. (are you?) If I am "washed" (in Jesus Blood) and totally cleansed, I want to show my appreciation and do what I can for Him out of thanksgiving and certain gratitude. Not live a life of forced guilt, and "non-acceptance" and fear . . . Going to Church of whatever "brand or flavor" is irrelevant. What counts' is Your belief, and only belief in what Christ has done for YOU!

Yes, we Are Still Sinners, but NOT in **God's eyes**, just in our own. We are Now His Holy Children. (But only after we accept what Jesus has done for us.) I Peter 2: 9 in the King James Version says *"You are a chosen people a royal priesthood, an holy nation peculiar people"* In the New International Version it is put like this 2:9 *"But you are a chosen people, a royal priesthood, a holy nation, God's special possession, that you may declare the praise of Him who called you out of darkness into His marvelous light."*

I have since done additional papers on these two main topics in the Bible and I have not made any of my own determinative conclusions as to the outcome. I just let scripture define itself. (ya that's some of that Hermeneutic-stuff) In a summarized sort, let me clarify what I have found,

1. John 3:16 *"For God so loved the world that he gave his only begotten son, that whosoever believes in him would not perish but have everlasting life.*
2. Romans 3:23 *"For all have sinned and <u>come short</u> of the glory of God."*
3. Romans 6:23 *"For the wages of sin is death but the gift of God is eternal life through Jesus*
4. *Christ our Lord. "Hebrews 9:22 . . . and without the shedding of blood there is no forgiveness of sins"*

If we just read only those few verses, and believed that the Bible is absolutely true, and that God does exist. How can anyone say that they have a part in assisting God to get themselves to eternal life in Glory? We can't. And you know what? I Never expected to be able to prove my point, but this story of my life/death proves it. And that is good enough for me. And I hope for you too.

If you do, or don't want to believe in God or the Bible, there is No point in reading this book, except for the quips and anecdotes. I will prove God's existence and his character, and if you don't want to believe me in this book. "Bye bye Now." Have a Nice life, down here, cause that's all your gonna get. Really! On the other side, You have to be ready or ELSE! That's not me talking, but God.

We can go a little farther now (in this book-not a doctrinal thesis). The book of I John, itself clearl nullifies that proclamation that we (born-again) believers need to confess our sins, because it simply states that our sins are *gone!* I John 3: 9 *"Whosoever is born of God doth not commit sin, for his seed remains in him, and he cannot sin, because he is born of God."* **What?** That's what it says. I sure didn't write something like that, only God's authority through John the Apostle, (probably Jesus own mortal brother-but that is Not a confirmed fact).

Many people (Jew or Gentile alike) whether they are "deep or not" into the scriptures; have heard the words. *"As far away as the east is from the west"* found in the book of Psalm 103:12. The book of Hebrews stresses emphatically in 9: 24 where it states *"For Christ is not entered into the holy place made with hands, which are the figures of the true, but into heaven itself, now to appear in the presence of God, for us."*

V25: *Nor yet that he should offer himself often, as the high priest entereth into the holy place every year with the blood of others;*

V26: *For then must he often have suffered since the foundation of the world. But now ONCE, in the end of the ages, hath he appeared to put away sin by the sacrifice of himself.*

The simple word **ONCE** should say enough. I can't keep asking for more forgiveness, of the sin that has already been paid for; and is deemed by God as Gone, Forgiven. {East-west}.

Yes I still sin, Yes I Am guilty. But washed and cleansed by His Holy Righteous pure blood. The sin has been paid for; it IS Now the consequences that I have to deal with here on this earth. Not the guilt of the sin, itself for eternity.

And if you are of Jewish heritage, and don't like all of this "Jesus is God" stuff; Just remember that almost all of the first "Christians" on earth were Jew's, including Jesus himself. (interesting-No?)

Here is my one question to you, (the reader) *"And the peace of God, which passes all understanding, shall keep you hearts and minds through Christ Jesus"* Philippians 4: 7. And I don't care what religion or maybe no religion you may be; do you have that PEACE? I can now say that "I honestly do." And there is nothing more precious to me, on this earth.

I couldn't go back into "ritualism" after that, or any, other religions teachings that rely on some "performance for acceptance." True Christianity teaches "acceptance-to be accepted" We accept Christ's invitation to receive him by trusting that His blood has washed us **clean** from our sins; and then we are totally accepted by HIM. That's IT! Really. That's what I had learned, that I was missing from all of my Lutheran teachings was, A FULL heart commitment, with None of my own accomplishments or procedures assisting Him in my salvation. How could a person be so mean to Jesus the Holy Son of God, to believe or think that they can help the almighty sovereign God of this universe get them to heaven? He Did It ALL! By HIMSELF!

If this turns you off, and you think that this "bible stuff" is a waste . . . Just wait 'till you take your last breath. Do you really believe (oh I said the "unthinkable-believe) that when your "done on this" earth that you are good for no more than worm food or fertilizer? Please. Even an atheist has to see that they have more value than that, else, where did we get all these "feelings" from? {ethics, morals, conscience guilt, worry, fear} None of which are part of the "the strongest survive" mentality.

Back to the Future

Now back to my life & first death experience. After numerous individual and group meetings with different members of the faculty, and staff members, at New Tribes in Jackson Michigan, I decided that the only proper thing to do was for my new bride and me to leave, and not cause any dissension. (ya, the Bible talks about doing that sort of thing too). So I called up my parents and told them we were moving back to Wisconsin, then my dad offered to come over with an *EZ Haul* box style truck, and put all our stuff back in and we would go back home to Milwaukee.

I do have to include, that in our time over there, I needed a job, for our daily living needs, so I was able to get a beginners position (entry level) at a little local body shop, where I was taught a lot of valuable information, and some skills and techniques, as to how to repair body parts on cars and trucks. Learning how to spray paint, later helped me back at Oak Creek, to make "trade-ins" snowmobiles, and motorcycles look a lot nicer. It also had a "play" in that providence thing I told you about. (you'll see)

My darling wife Elsbeth and I were in full agreement as to the return; nevertheless, we were so dismayed at our lost opportunity to go overseas and serve. We obviously didn't know what the future held, but took life's blows as they occurred, one at a time.

PS., God never said a missionary had to live in a jungle, or wear a grass skirt either. (ha ha)

Chap. 9

My Dad's Dad

It was about a six-eight hour drive, (with Chicago traffic) going back to Milwaukee. My wife and I took turns driving the car behind my dad, who was driving the big box truck. It was probably some of the most valuable six hours of my life with my dad. He and I were talking about everything going on over in Michigan, this gave me the opportunity to explain, to my dad (who was Roman Catholic) how I had come from studying to be a Lutheran Minister, to finding that I was really going to hell, myself.

I know that it sure must have made a big impact on my father; I say this, because when we got back to Wisconsin, even he started attending church with us. He told me that he too had come to accept Christ as his Savior and trust that his sins had been completely paid for. And to this day he never misses fellowshipping at church, if he can help it, and he's now a spry eighty five year old, who even works at least three days a week at a grocery store in his little town . . . His doctor says that his health and wellbeing alone are miraculous.

Okay, so now we're back in Southeast Wisconsin, I returned to the motorcycle shop to work, and my wife worked there too, until she had the two boys, that I had told you about earlier. As our receptionist she had learned a lot about motorcycles and engines; because she also became a sort of "surrogate" parts person as well. Things were going along quite well and we were living in a nice little first floor apartment, part of an 8 family building. Not far from the apartment complex we lived in the first few months we were married. Out of concern for that young customer/friend Tom, who helped us move; I did what I could to contact him. Then he would come over to hang out, at our place . . . a lot. (newlyweds love that). But he was again, going down a path that was headed for destruction otherwise.

Yes, girls, my wife rode her own cycle too. As a matter of fact over the years she had several of them. All two stokes (stinky, noisy) and never so much as one of them ever even had electric start; only kick-start. Is that what you might label as a "real biker babe"? OK . . . Probably not.

Then one mid-summer, Wednesday night in 1975, I went down, as I had gone back to doing; to the "rap session" in Chicago, but I did convince a group of young customers and some friends to ride down with me on their bikes too. Included in this group was my forty seven year old father, who suddenly began to have an interest in what the Bible really had to say; and a young seventeen year old customer, who had just gotten his new Kawasaki two stroke 500 triple, from me, just a few days earlier.

Curves that Don't appeal

It was about 4:30 and six of us headed down for a nice ride and a "rap session" bible study, to boot. My dad's incentive to come, may have been the promise of "great coffee." He sooo . . . loved his coffee, and I told him that they had a lot and it and it was real good. See, in the W.W.II theater of war, when the guys weren't near a base, the only thing they could do was keep re-heating the same old grounds over and over. That got old "real quick" but what were their options?

Now it's a beautiful summer afternoon riding our cycles down the express-way then on to old US 41, which turns into the Eden's expressway, until we got to the house near two popular and busy roads in Chicago, called Montrose and Cicero ave. on the near north side of the city.

We all got off the ramp on the right, and came to a light to stop. I was in the lead, because I was the only one who knew how to get there. This is where it gets tricky. On that off ramp, there were multiple roads adjoining one-another just to the right of the off ramp itself. It is one of the "strangest" Intersections ever. What makes it all so interesting, is the big huge multi-columned bridge abutment for the Chicago "L" train that went just overhead. That's not so different, but it was on a 45 degree angle as well, heading toward downtown and those columns came very shortly after you make a double "snake" style turn to the left, you go south/southwest where the road "veers" to the right to cross and continue south. (got that?)

when the Good Times Don't Roll

After the light changed to green, I turned right and then I quickly proceeded into the far left lane, (almost immediately) as the light there was red. The others all did the same, and we waited there for a green light. When it changed, I took off, to the left, (not going extreme left onto another road that also adjoined, but the one headed more south-southwest, going under the "L" train columns. Everyone followed me including the newest young owner who was a couple of bikes behind me. He just couldn't prevent himself from showing off his new hot 500 Triple, and he really gave it a lot of throttle. First, being NOT used to the new bike, then not aware of the Y split of the two roads going south, then giving it way to much gas, he leaned way to far over and went down in the middle of the two southbound lanes.

All of this being unknown to me, as I had gone underneath the L train bridge abutment another five or six blocks and turned down the city street to go to the house. Well when nobody showed up behind me just as I'm turning onto the residential road, after those three curves that I had just taken. I suddenly realized that I now had no followers from our group behind me yet. I quickly turned around and went back, to see what was going on.

"O No," I screamed inside my helmet, the road was plugged tight with cycles and cars strewn all about. There was absolutely nobody moving. All behind and around that "L" train trestle. I rushed back as quick as I could get that Kawasaki H2 750 to go, and then I saw the kid laying in the middle of the road, and his bike in shambles up against the outside lane curb. But what really brought panic to my eyes, was when I saw that my dad was down also. Just before the bridge abutment and column; just behind the young driver.

I slammed on the brakes as quick as possible, on the north bound side trestle and then I ran as fast as I could, and said to myself "Thank the Lord, everybody was now standing up." The young man's bike was really rough, but run–able and we got it to the house of the lady teacher. Now my dad's bike was a whole different story.

Coming up to the incident after the curve, he realized he had three options

1. run over the "kid", laying in the middle of the road,
2. veer off to the left and drive into the front of an oncoming garbage truck (no median right there,) or
3. hit the bridge brick column. He chose the column Head on. By the way, this will come into much greater significance a little later, and YES, we all had helmets on in this situation.

The whole front end of my dad's bike was literally broken away from the rest of the cycle, the cables and brake hose was all that was holding the whole thing together. So just to expedite things as best as possible, I slid the "triple tree" shaft back up into the front frame housing and trickled the bike, the best I could, holding onto the forks themselves just to steer, and get it the remaining six block to the lady's house. It was a challenge that I sure never had planned ever experiencing, either.

Believe it or not; I thanked God that No one was severely hurt, just some "road rash," and a whole lot of ego damage. The young fella even drove his bike back to Milwaukee, that night. So "all's well that ends well" was our mantra for the evening. Whew!!

One interesting little note, if you drive motorcycles and then ever had to ride on the back with someone else driving, there is nothing much more fearful and downright scarier than being that passenger. Agreed? My dad had to ride all the way back, behind me. I still hear about that ride to this day. As he says "Pure Horror."

The "infamous" *Pipeline*

When came the Memorial weekend in 1975, which was about all we ever got to get any time off in the motorcycle business, especially in spring or summer. Hank, the owner, and a few other employees and my wife and I, took a load of dirt-bikes way up to the north/north-east corner of Wisconsin. We knew a couple of fellas from the cycle shop, as customers and now friends. They were Tom's friends first, who let us stay in their little "hunting" style cabin that was pretty far back in the woods.

We had a couple of cars and trucks loaded with food, riding gear, and two motorcycle trailers that held three bikes each; behind each vehicle. Atv's were just coming out and they weren't quite "the stuff" for the kind of riding that we were going to be doing. It was about a four hour drive to get there from Milwaukee, and when we finally found the place and settled in, it was time to hit the sack, so we would be ready the next morning.

That beautiful spring day, when we all got up and unloaded the bikes from the trailers, we put our riding gear on and helmets and took off. We weren't "real" sure of just exactly where to go, to get this "Pipeline" trail start. All of our directions were verbal (No GPS back then) and after a few of the wrong little fire lane roads, we found a 200 foot wide and very hilly gulch-wheeled rutty trail going off to the left. So we all took off on our strong torque fast long travel dirt-bikes. These were some real intense type riding conditions.

The "natural gas" pipeline runs up to the U.P. of Michigan, from down in central Wisconsin. Absolutely every kind of terrain, water, mud, sand, silt, and lots of rocks that you could imagine traveling, came to meet us on the other side of each hill, rock pile, or curve. For off-road, dirt trail riders, you couldn't ask for better. Occasionally the big huge pipe itself was even exposed.

The Good Times Roll—too fast

The extended weekend was now over. We were loading everything up into the vehicles. My "poo" (not chocolate brown either) Ford Torino wagon, and the other guys trucks and trailers. Here is the part that I just "growled" over. I was pulling a pretty new three place motorcycle trailer that was painted sky-blue and beige. The Kawasaki's were (obviously) all lime green. Alright I was not very "incognito" Okay? But hey the mud coming off the cycles matched; no the mud looked better than the brown station wagon.

Back to the growl. We had been driving, in a small five vehicle "caravan" (NO—not a Dodge minivan). We were about fifteen to twenty miles south of Green Bay, Wis., on the expressway, which happened to be packed with cars (40-60% Illinois plates.) and we were *ALL* going about fifteen miles an hour over the speed limit.(ya ya-ok-I know). There really wasn't much choice, either. All three lanes were about the same, and close to "bumper-bumper." When *all of a sudden* there's a set of red-lights flashing behind me. I thought what? Maybe a bike's tie down straps came loose, or something. So when I finally could get over into the right lane and then on the shoulder, this State Patrol officer, who was following very close behind, got out of his squad and sauntered over to my driver's window. "Yes officer?" I chirped after rolling my window down. He just said "Let me see your license" "Yes sir" I wimped. "What's wrong sir?" I continued. He didn't even look at me, just my license, and said . . . "Do You Know How Fast YOU were Going?" "I was just stuck in with all of the traffic sir, and I think we were all going a little over seventy mph.

91

"Yes—Do you know how far over the limit that is?" He parceled out to me, that questions. "Yes sir, its sixty miles an hour" You are being ticketed for fifteen over the limit." He snapped. "But sir, we were all going the same speed, why Me.?"

"Look, pal, If you decide that you want to come back up here, and fight this in court. I win "hands down. Because when the judge asks me if I'm sure that it was You, and that was the speed. I will be totally safe. How many all brown, with a blue motorcycle trailer, and three lime green motorcycles, could I possible confuse that with? Otherwise there was just too many to be able to separately identify." "So I'm taking the toll for everybody?" In a pleading voice. "Yup, sorry kid. That's life"

Heaven: full of {dirt?}

Funniest thing, a year or so later, I was sharing with one of the guys that we had just met, about the ride he took with us on the pipeline. He just couldn't imagine anything better or more fun to do than ride those fifty to sixty miles on his new Kawasaki dirt-bike, either. But there were a whole lot of challenges, up there.

So now, I was doing him a favor, after we closed down the motorcycle store on a Saturday night. He had just put a tall fiberglass roof on his full size van, for his mother-in-law, to be able to ride with them. Only problem was, his Ford van was all dark (pooh) brown, and this new huge roof piece was fiberglass off (yucky) white. Euwww.

So I gladly offered to paint it for him. (You know-Mr. "experienced body man"-ha ha) He agreed, because it couldn't look any worse when I got done with it, so he surmised. Hey, It did come out looking pretty darn OK; that's all I'll say. Ya' just had to squint, in low light.

But it took us five to six hours and meanwhile, me and my big mouth, started telling him about our time in Jackson Michigan. Somehow God got into the picture too. (Huh-surprise?) He said he agreed with everything that I told him, just that he didn't want to go to Heaven, because it seemed to be "Real Boring" to him. "Just to sit around on clouds, waving our wings and white gowns and saying Praise God, Praise God" He told me that wouldn't be his "cup of tea" (his words were a little stronger than that). I then explained that God didn't go through "all that", for us just to sit around and be bored and sing psalms, and playing harps. So I told him that Heaven is more like the most wonderful place to be and doing the most wonderful activities, and his eyes got wide, when I told him that for him heaven was "probably" like the pipeline, or a motocross race track, that's up here in lower Wisconsin. He then said "count me in" I to want to get saved and have a Great Eternity, if it's going to be that good.

See. I didn't tell him anything wrong. It is just that Heaven is talked about a lot, just not in detail, besides the book of Revelation. (which described things in the "genre" that they knew how back then.

Heaven is basically the most exquisite place that one could imagine. For me a field full of (Kaw's)? I just don't know if they can pave dirt with gold? (hmm . . . God must be a Kawasaki dealer, 'cuz, it says in the Book of Psalms 50:10 the He owns the cattle (Kaws") on a thousand hills. (look—I just can't help it; you'll see-really.

Chap. 10

Green with Envy

Life was going along pretty darn well again (heard that before, huh?) And I was really enjoying each day, selling Kawasaki's. It IS True! When you do what you love, you Never work. I started putting a lot of ads on the local radio stations, that I would sometimes scribble on the sides of the cardboard covering the motorcycle crates, (hey, who knows when *inspiration* hits?) and the radio sales people, would just love it, when I gave the script on a 2x3' piece of torn off motorcycle crate. Everybody at the station (WKLH FM) sure enjoyed the fun in that.

For those of you who maybe don't know or remember, Kawasaki's team racing colors are Green/lime. But none the less, green. And being in Milwaukee, when I had the announcer on the popular classic-rock station "robustly" read the script. It ended like this "Oak Creek MotorSports and Kawasaki, will {turn-'em GREEN with envy.} Yes I got a few calls from a motorcycle company (who'll remain anonymous) representative that tried to convince me that talk like that wouldn't "work". They were Milwaukee's motorcycle heritage. NOT Kawasaki's. All I could say in response to that, was, "Aw . . . !"

Cops' on Kaws!

For any one old enough to remember the popular T.V. Show *Chips,* with the dashing Eric Estrada; maybe you did or maybe not also notice, but all of those California Highway Patrol (CHIPS) motorcycles just happened to be Kawasaki's. What! Oh No . . . Yesses. They were, Kawasaki's cycles that were and still are made smack dab in the middle of the U.S.A. Right in Lincoln, Nebraska. At that time already for over ten years and they were selling police bikes to municipalities all over the country.

So guess who got a *bid invitation* for Police Motorcycles for all of Milwaukee County. Yup-you guessed, right. I called the police division of Kawasaki in Atlanta, Ga. And talked with the national police sales division rep., Henry Shnittker. We analyzed their specifications and bid request, and then sent in a proposal.

About a month or so went by and we got a written notice of a hearing for the police motorcycle allocation that the county was shortly going to place an order for. We were WAAAYYY . . . less money than the local competition and Kawasaki hadn't gone in and out of bankruptcy several times either, like some others we know. The cost saving to taxpayers for the price of the cycles, and the annual up keep, that was well recorded, was spectacular.

The national rep. Henry, came up to the meeting with me and we sat there with quiet anticipation in the committee meeting room, which was packed. With three different unions leaders and minions. Boy did they put up a ruckus, about losing all their jobs, and business for the county.

So after a week went by the letter came, informing us that due to "adverse pressure" they decided to stay with the same old same old (my words not the letters). Could you just imagine if a Hardly executive got stopped by a cop on a Kawasaki, in Milwaukee County? Wooow that would have really hurt.

A lot of people already know that Wisconsin touts itself as America's Dairy land. Which is what you see at the top of every auto and truck license plate, which is imbedded in a nice rural farm scene. So, I thought to myself, well I might be dying early doing this but, eh . . . what the heck. So I had many billboards placed all over greater Milwaukee area that showed a Green motorcycle on one half, and a green Kawasaki Jet Ski on the other. With the bold announcement "We're known for our *Kaw's-not our hoggs*. That is the kind of attention that an advertiser wants. But it seemed like it might be bringing me closer to the (my) end, as well. There were just some folks here in town that couldn't appreciate my sense of value, and humor. To say the least some of their biker customer's didn't appreciate me at all.

Hank, the single stock holder of the motorcycle shop, saw that the business was being so successful despite the "all other brands" influence, and he was so pleased that my sales were excelling so well beyond anyone's expectations that he decided to draw up all the necessary papers, that upon his death (be it of injury, or illness or whatever) I would be the holder of a policy that would pay for the company's inventory and equipment, and even the buildings as well, so that the dealership would continue on and one day become mine as the owner. (p.s. That didn't go far)

Just to let you sales people know. I <u>never</u> got so much as ONE commission check for all of those sales. NO not One. My motivation wasn't dollar signs. I did however get an incredible "perk" that was worth more than money. For their business advancement, <u>often times</u> Kawasaki would award us one of these nice two week trips to some exotic location around the world. And we had to go annually to places like, LasVegas, New Orleans, Lake Tahoe, etc. Ya, it was a rough life, but like *they* say "somebody had "ta" do it." And so we were "wined and dined" very well, because of our accomplishments in Kawasaki sales.

Evinrude, Arctic Cat, and Polaris, would have really nice dealer meeting as well, but having just come back from say, Monte Carlo, Paris, Munich, Athens, London, or some other exotic location, a local dinner hall just didn't do the same for us. But we went to see the new product and check out the new programs as well.

The Good, Times were Rolling along <u>so well</u>, and we were selling a lot of Kawasaki, Arctic Cat and Polaris snowmobiles and some of the new three wheeled things called ATV's. But then the

Kawasaki factory rep named "Jet" (Gary) Johnson, came to Oak Creek MotorSports and told us of a brand new product Kawasaki was testing and most likely going to come out with. It was made for fresh or salt water. He wanted to find out if we were interested, & we were Evinrude and Silver Line boat dealers already. It would be called a *Jet Ski*. You would stand or kneel on it and ride all around in the water, almost right up on to the beach. My parents; **don't forget**, lived on a lake, so when they (Jet Ski's) did come out, not only did they show it to us first in the Midwest, on a trailer, we took out to my parents lake and we got to drive it all around. Was that thing ever fun and exciting! And now we could let the "Good Times Splash" as well.

The factory rep. "Jet" told me that, this was the very first Jet Ski driven on the water in the state of Wisconsin. We started selling Jet Skis and it took a couple of years but they did take off in sales too. Because here in southeast Wisconsin, we have a lot of inland lakes as well as that one big" puddle" called Lake Michigan. Our dealership was even invited to come down to this brand new "venture "on the lake, (Michigan) and put on a show for all the guests to enjoy watching us ride. This venue was called Summer *Fest*. Myself and another young high-school aged fella, we called *Skippy*, who worked summers for us, would go down and put on a couple of different shows throughout the day. And the rest of the time we could just "hang-out" and enjoy the fest for ourselves, for free!

一番

Kawasaki
ICHIBAN

What . . . ?

Now, *The Good Times* weren't just rolling along, they were "steamin". And at the 1982 Kawasaki dealer meeting in Vegas, there were about 3000 people in the convention hall, and we had a great opening show, and the next day we saw all the new models that were coming out, and accessories plus so many aftermarket venders that were invited to the dealer show as well. At the second great big evening dinner & show, before the special celebrities that they usually had for us dealers; they would put on a great big awards presentation, Hank and I each excused ourselves right after we ate, so we'd be back for the awards presentation on time, and we went to the restroom in the long hall foyer, before the evening festivities really began.

Just as we were about to exit back into the hallway, the Vice President and Regional Sales Manager of Kawasaki Motors Corp. USA. were approaching us, as we both thought that they were going to use the facilities as well. But they insistently stopped us in the door-way and reached out their hands to congratulate us . . . huh . . . Why? What for? We were . . . quite successful in the bathroom? "What is this all about" we both queried.

You've got what kind of itch?

"You, Guys" have just become the **Nation's Largest Kawasaki** Dealer" "The Whaat?" was our response, who us a nice little dealership in Milwaukee? "How did we do that?" We both asked. "You sold more product than any other Kawasaki dealer in America! You are *ICHIBAN*! (Japanese for **#1**" They "somewhat" proudly announced.

Just as we were about to exit back into the hallway, the Vice President and Regional Sales Manager of Kawasaki Motors Corp. USA, were approaching us in the door-way and reached out their hands to congratulate us . . . huh? . . . Why? . . . What for? We were successful in the bathroom? "What is this all about" we both queried. They did it on the "down-lo." Am I now proud or ashamed?

Festivities really began. Just as we were about to exit back into the hallway, the Vice President and Regional Sales Manager, insistently approached us. We thinking that they too had to use the facilities, we backed to the side, as they still came forward to us. They then said the "most unimaginable and incredible" words; as they reached out to shake our (washed) hands.

You've got what kind of itch?

"You, "Guys have just become the **Nation's Largest Kawasaki** Dealer" "Whaat?" was our response, who us a nice little dealership in Milwaukee? How did we do that? "You sold more product than anyone else in America. You are *ICHIBAN*! (Japanese for #1" They "somewhat" proudly announced. Out here in front of the "john"?

"What the heck?" I mused. They gave that beautiful 18 carat gold and diamond ring and a very "classy" inscribed plaque, to us in the door-way of the men's bathroom. (Anybody from Kawasaki-don't ever do something like that again-please) But nobody like us should have ever received that award, it always went to California, or maybe Texas, but Milwaukee Wisconsin. Not even one of the big Chicago dealers? They just didn't know how the reaction was going to be, so they did it on the "down-lo." Am I now proud or ashamed? The men's bathroom? Maybe they were "intimidated" by another motorcycle company? Please. But hey **WE DID IT!** "Nothin's" cooler than that. Now just wait 'til Milwaukee hears about this. They will be shooting at me, after these ads come out. Ask yourself this question, if "everybody" loves Hardley so much, who was buying ALL Those Kawasaki's in Milwaukee? Hmmm. And they weren't all *Jet Ski's*.

The Largest Kawasaki dealer in the United States of America!

Right here in Milwaukee, Wisconsin; Hardly's home town; what does that tell ya? You wanna talk about Pride! That was Us. Alright.

We sold 806 new Kaw's that year. (Ya I was the only salesperson. If we had more maybe we could have hit 1000. And then . . .)

Life just couldn't get much better than that. Like I said we were on a full steam roll! So '83 came and went, with a lot of sales, and we were one of the top ten dealer of America year after year, so we were ICHIBAN dealers again, which actually went on for eight years in a row. Then 1984 & 1985 came and went with great success, and we were starting a good season in the spring of 1986.

Elsbeth and I had another little boy, just before Christmas, in December of 1982 and everybody was healthy and safe. As the boys were growing up, and they had it really *really* good, with, now "Uncle Hank" taking care of many of their interests. He loved those two boys, a lot.

A few more worldwide Ichiban trips, including taking my wife to Rio DeJaneiro, Brazil, and then to those Iguassu waterfalls; that, remember make Niagara look like a dripping faucet. Those are the falls that are in the middle of the South American continent, where that "Rap Session" lady-Lois and her husband Don were missionaries. We went to Hawaii, Acapulco, Vegas, Tahoe, & New Orleans. My oldest son even got to come with us to a few of the dealer meeting trips to Vegas, and Hawaii. On the trip to Hawaii, we were way-laid at San Francisco, because of a huge, "hundred years" storm, attacking the Hawaiian Islands. So they said we'd have at least fifteen to eighteen hours to wait.

Remember I said that Hank was a very giving person. He called up to the gateway at the airports, and had, a taxi and the driver (of course) give us a three hour tour of the whole city of San Francisco, and going over the Golden Gate Bridge, as well. How would you have liked that taxi fare? Hank pulled out a lot of bills from his wallet, for that one. Owuuu. But was it beautiful, and interesting.

On another Ichiban trip, to Italy, Hank and I had been with the other twenty or so, for a few days. We were staying in a real old elegant (what else?—Kawasaki) hotel, on the third floor, our room was facing the Del a Rosa, a main city road, near the center of Rome.

It was a busy downtown, street a few blocks away from the Vatican. Our beds were up against the "outside" wall, of the room, and there were windows on either side of the two beds.

"Getting Bombed?" in Italy

Somewhere around three am. There came a huge sudden staggering **explosion**, and sprinkling noise on the outside of our wall and the windows, crackling. We were both in a deep sleep, after having enjoyed a big beautiful dinner and some fantastic Italian wine. (more than one or two glasses—I think).massive bright light just across the street at about the same floor level as we. What was that all about? We both wondered. Do we stay? Do we go, maybe downstairs? We had no idea. So we both got dressed and took the stairs down to the lobby, where they were trying to calm all the guests down.

They told us that it was the third floor and the whole front of the brick hotel building just across the street was now all gone. All the bricks were now laying all over the sidewalks like, war rubble, and parked and now flattened cars below. "What happened, was it may be a natural gas leak and explosion, or what?" we all asked.

Then a man ran into the lobby, and told us that the Israeli Ambassador's room had just been blown up and they didn't know how many had been killed, but they knew some had died.

Just a little alert: Nobody knows how much time they've got. That bomb could have been easily in the floor above or below us, or we could have been in that hotel, and died or been severely hurt in Rome, Italy, on vacation You Just Never Know. Give that some thought.

On another trip to Acapulco, (this time it was Kawasaki Snowmobiles, (Acapulco-snowmobiles? Hey it was an exotic dealer trip not a snowmobile ride). We went out para-sailing (which was a pretty new thing back then.). If you ever get the chance; you have got to try it, Para-sailing is absolutely Spectacular! We then took a day trip up to Taxco, Mexico, where they mine silver and make beautiful silver jewelry. Yes, I was getting closer to broke, again. But this time; not from a Sailfish.

School—Again?

We, as husband and wife, and parents did a lot of research and decided to home school our two boys, that we love so much and wanted nothing but "the best" for. We did this through seventh grade and then chose a really good Christian Grade/High School for them to attend. I just loved meeting their teachers, and professors because I learned a lot about what they were learning too, and the so many different understanding and insights they each had.

For example, {atheist-skip this part} when I went to school, we were taught that science was an accumulation of known & maybe prior unknown facts, that could deride a conclusion. Now, if you watch TV like some of the science or history shows, they often announce that "scientist now believe . . ." believe? That {this-this—or that} must be the conclusion. SCIENCE? Really! That's what it is now called Science? I was raised to learn that was nothing more than "conjecture." And how can you believe in a black hole you can't see, but speculate on (through some "non validated" facts). And you can't believe in God? Maybe we just don't want any conviction. (from "outside")

Both of my sons, had, in their juniors and seniors class, an extremely intelligent science professor who also happened to believe in the Bible. (get that) Simply & clearly explained how so-called "science" could easily and plainly NOT be correct, in the area of "age of the earth, the universe; & how it must have been created after the "Big Bang". But by using simple math, and "absolute" facts. It is known that the Sun diminishes one foot per earth year. So just by multiplying that foot per year in reverse, in just so many million-Not Billion years the Sun would be absorbing a good portion of this earth itself. Rendering it a "melted mess" not a planet. Oh! But let's believe that it's "science" so they say. And then we won't have to believe in God. Surreee . . . I just love *science? (tists?)* That, when a new revelation comes about, they just ADD another billion years to their summation. Please–get REAL and Actual!

I discussed this concept and a few others, of the school's faculty, as well. I have questioned evolutionist on this so called understanding, with only the slightest variation and certainly no alacrity in their retort, with "well respected" (I think) Science engineers, and professors. The question is simple. "Let's just say that genetic evolution is correct, why has there been no evidence in cross–over of species; but more importantly, if evolution uses the "survival of the fittest" mantra for its evidence, then how do you explain,_**1**.conscience **2.** guilt or **3.** Worry, **4.** fear, or any other "self–deprecating emotional and psychological condition?" The conversation usually ended right about there. They claim that they will still "choose the "speculative science;" as their conclusion to the beginning of the universe. They'd "Swear to God", they're right. No kidding. (ha ha) Even Darwin, only labeled his writing as a *"Theory of Evolution"* hmmm talk about *having some faith?*

Science IS pretty neat though, if you think about it. The more they search into the universe, the more "IT" baffles everyone. By learning how much more pervasive and by light years extensive the universe is, than even this centuries first astronomers first thought.

Isn't that "cool", how it shows God's "Pure" love must be even more incredible? What . . . You say? If He did all this (which I believe He did) for us . . . way down here on this tiny little spec called earth. Just imagine how much he could love YOU!

Chap. 11

Road Kill! Dead, Really?—Dead.

Now, here IT IS; what you've really been waiting for, I'm pretty sure. Yes I keep saying that 'cause to each of us it's something else. No . . . ? Yup? It was spring of 1986 getting close to full summer fun, and things were going great. As another aside, I should tell you first. My wife, my dad, and sons, & I were all attending a nice little Bible church about a mile from our house, and I, of course partook in the communion, and preaching, and Sunday School teaching, and occasional funeral and or wedding.

And I guess I must have had a "knack" at talking to young adults. About twelve years earlier, I had some young teens who went to the church and even some neighbor kids would come to our house every Friday night about 8: 00 till 10: pm, and we would sit around our family room and go through different books of the Bible, and the whole thing kept growing and growing. (No not groaning) ha-ha. (could this be another one of those "Rap sessions-Oh No) Here one of my best laughs in life, was there, during a prayer that I asked one of the young fellas named Randy, to open us with. Because we were going to be studying in the book of Romans chapter 5, whose "sub theme" is patience, which is what I told the kids we would be studying "tonight" So I asked Randy to open us in prayer before we got started. This is his quote:

"Lord you are going to teach us all about patience tonight; and my prayer to you is LORD! I Want Patience and I Want It NOW!"

Ya that IS right where the prayer ended. We were all laughing so hard, none of us could contain ourselves. Note: If we ask anything in God, that's His will, we have the answer coming to us.

I must confess, that repeatedly, over all those years, I proclaimed to those kids, that "there is "no such thing" as an **accident,** with God," How can there be? He knows everything already, Latin (Omniscient). They all saw what I mean about "providence" and our lives were already a "past tense" thing with God; because He is Outside of time. Our lives aren't controlled by Him, but he knew and knows the outcome to each occurrence in our lives. "Remember: Everything past <u>NOW</u>!—is already part of history." Heavy; huh?

I was counseling a lot of the adolescents and tried to help them get through their teen years, dealing with their parents, or foster parents, even the other pastors' kids, plus class-mates & teachers. One young set of "love-birds" came to me in 1985 and said that they wanted to get married, if I would do the honors of performing the service for them and go through the "necessary" pre-marital counseling with them. I immediately said "Yes!" I loved both of these kids, and they knew it. So we went on through the counseling classes and they kept me aware of where, when, and what was going on in all of the ceremonial activities to come. The date was set for Saturday JULY <u>5th.</u> We were all getting ready and excited (it was going to be my first wedding, to lead alone) Then on Tuesday July <u>1st,</u> at 6:02 in the afternoon; on a hot and sunny and very bright clear day. Everything in my life completely changed!

Please forgive this next part of the story; I'm relying on the eyewitness statement from those who saw the whole incident. As well as going by all of the employee and witness testimonial statements. As I'm/was told it is typically common, that I would have/had absolutely NO memory of that late afternoon, or the next fourteen days, for that matter.

I had set the business hours years ago, Mon. & Fri. 10-7, Tues. Wed. Thur. 10-6, and Sat. 10-3. Sun. CLOSED. Six days a week since college. As employees, we were often there, well before opening sometimes much later then close. So in a groaning metaphoric request, I had asked the Bible-study gal Lois, down in Chicago, years earlier, about that once. As I complained about the sixty-seventy sometimes almost eighty hour work week. She simply looked me in the eye and asked "How many days did it take God to create the world?" "Six" I said. "So then, what the . . . blank (she didn't cuss) makes you think you're so much better than Him. He only got one day off, too." I slunk off, with my mouth shut tight.

That Tuesday, which I guess had been a slightly less hectic day than usual, allowed us to close right at 6:00, on the dot. I walked to the front of the store with the other employees, and locked the front door, hopped on my brand new model, "dealer demo", it was a whole new type of Kawasaki. Called the Concourse, ZG1000/A1, a "sport-touring" style bike. Of course those 4 cylinder liquid cooled cylinder fired right up. I then turned and waved goodbye to all the employees, and got right on that big 4 lane highway, and headed north for home. Just one mile north, there is a very large/busy intersection, that has a high use—on/off ramp from I-94 just to its east about a half mile, and it is a normally active road anyhow, especially when it is a weekday afternoon, and so many people are coming from the city to the suburbs to get home, or where-ever their lives needed to go.

The road to "perdition"?

I had taken this road straight home for over thirteen years now, so you could easily assume, I was quite familiar with all the surroundings; to say the least. So, I apparently was in the left hand lane, my bookkeeping gal Kara, a cute little brunette, who was in the right hand lane now next to me. My cousin Ruth was our receptionist at that time, and she was a pretty long haired brunette too with a super smile, cheerful looks and great demeanor. Those two gals presence sure helped to get the guys attention, and head for the office to buy "that" bike. (Hey common, that's business, marketing, OK?) Besides everything else, they were a couple of real sharp gals, with all of the paper work, and government forms, and the cycle cloths and accessories as well. One of the younger single guys who went to our church needed a job, so I had him working for us; setting up motorcycles out of the crates. His own bike that he was riding home on, had just turned to the left into a raised curb median left turn lane. His back was now away from Kara and I, who were going straight ahead.

Many of the witnesses said, that I must have looked in my mirror and saw another motorcycle pulling up in my lane behind me, so as I'm slowing way down, and coming to the now red light, I veered to the left even further, to give him room in that lane with me. Yes, it is legal to have two motorcycles share a lane, under Wisconsin law. So we just sat their idling our bikes while we waited for the red light to turn green, we were both the first ones in that lane. It was a pretty long light with the left turn indicators switching on ahead of the straight on lanes.

"BAMM! CRASH!" (sorry no sound effects)There was No screeching of tires from braking sounds at all, or alerting sounds of any sort. Normal traffic noise **were** all anyone heard. The wallop and crunching sound at the instant impact, extremely startled the biker next to me as he immediately looked down and to his left where he heard the noise. He turned just to see his left leg almost get sheared off by the right front fender of the colliding car, and he saw that I was no longer where I had been sitting, but now my motorcycle was protruding into the front end of this old standard four door sedan, that kept speeding by him, right into the center of all the lanes. The "instantaneous" crash, gave absolutely **No** one any warning to anyone. "Thanks God", none of the cross traffic got struck by this vehicular concoction. The initial impact was over in just a few seconds.

In that split second, I was struck, by a car that was going at such a high rate of speed; (as the witnesses and police said) that it was almost fifty miles an hour. He obviously had no intention of slowing down or braking, when he hit me. And then sent the motorcycle right into the red lights of that intersection and all of that cross traffic. That old four door sedan that had just hit me at that "deadly" speed, sent me flying upward through the air. "Three stories" (come on) high, (if one can believe thirty-three different witnesses, that are all part of the police reports). And I didn't even have a cape on! (bummer)

As I've said I'm a smaller short "slightly overweight" guy five feet six and a half inches" (pre-accident) 200 + lbs. whose wife is "one incredible cook, and better yet, a spectacular desert maker. I'm sure she married me just to be her "taste tester," OK, we'll leave that right there. But that "aerial score" that I performed must have been quite a bizarre sight to see). Like I have said earlier. On the way down I proceeded to make two reverse summers-salts, (get jealous high-divers). I landed on the roof of the car that had just crashed into me, and then I caved in that roof right over the driver's head with my feet. But then, they said that I bounced way up and landed on the car roof with my feet again, a second time, but then my feet flew forward, and I hit the roof with my rump, and I bounced and landed on that spot, one more time. (Back breaking land? You'll love this part later; believe me). It must have felt like being on a teeter-totter (when they were still allowed to be in parks and play grounds) if the person on the other end jumps or falls off at the bottom, leaving you to come smashing to earth on the teeter-totter board (great pain—could lead to a say "broken back?")

come fly with me

I proceeded to slide down the front of driver side windshield, and then I actually flew with my full face" helmeted" head draped to the left, (standing up, not horizontal like superman-darn). One of the several policemen from the two adjoining municipalities (they all knew me instantly, when they were "on lunch" or break they would kind-a-like to hang out at the "big" toy store too) took a tape measure in hand, said that I had flown 99 feet, while the other department's officer made his report at 98.75'. I couldn't even get a "lousy 100"

The DOA Who Made It!

feet, maybe for frequent flier mileage, NO? Boy they couldn't even make it 100 feet. Oh well that's" life–NO wait; That's Death!

But you do have to admit to yourself, that flying close to 100 feet through the air, with no landing net, just pavement, couldn't have been a very enjoyable experience, for any one. I hope I was "out" by then. Please let me tell you; that part wasn't fun. Again remember "so I'm told".

Probably 40 to 50 cars, waiting to go all different directions, at that intersection, each driver now had their life put on hold; while mine was ending. Some needed to do business, or was just excited about something/someone, other interests; they all had a good reason for being right there–right then. (you'll see) The whole intersection now came to a full screeching halt, with a male who's (full face helmeted) body laid on the far side of the intersection, still in the traffic lane. **"Stone Dead"** There was a motorcycle now deeply imbedded into the front end of this old car, like an oversized hood ornament, (ya Hardley lover's would say "that's where they belong) and the car was now blocking the whole intersection, in all directions. I was even told that the driver of the car that hit me, so much as <u>never</u> ever, even put his brakes on at all, and that's why it kept going across the intersection, and why there was no screeching tires or any skid marks on the road.

Believe it or not, he almost got me again the second time with the front end of my own motorcycle that finally stopped the car just a few feet away from my body, for the second time in 15–20 seconds. But hey, I was dead already anyhow. Could you just imagine, (Hardley riders will love this one too even my own Kaw' almost tried to kill me. (What?)

how to get someones attention

Between screams and panic, car tires screeching to a halt, trying their all not to hit each other, people began scurrying all around, now to and fro, in complete chaos and bewilderment. There was one man, in a really nice suit, who was just coming off the expressway going home from a day's work downtown, he was heading west when he got to the intersection. And he was going cross-ways to my direction. Thank God, that he did stop immediately; despite the chance of getting rear-ended himself, by the car behind him trying to make the light. I was told that he "jumped" out of his car quickly, and came running over to my body. I was lying on the asphalt, "face down" **dead** and clearly motionless. He then rolled me over, and proceeded to take my (heavily scraped in the front) full face helmet off my head. He thought that he would have to do something like C.P.R., but never having been through an event like this, he was very unsure of himself, initially. Then analyzing the situation, he deemed it crucial to begin some form of resuscitation. Which had it not been for a full face helmet, there would have been no face left to do any kind of CPR on. He said that all he saw was lots of blood gushing out of my mouth. He put his ear to my nose and mouth and tried to see if I Did or Did Not have any hint of breath or a Pulse! Laying right there, in his arms I was "stone cold" <u>DEAD</u>! Ready to meet my maker. I Do thank God, to this day for that man and his "Good Samaritan" values, and the training that he had to do C.P.R. prior.

I have got to admit, every time I think of this and or talk about it I get chills. Because after I finish describing this location to you, now some 26 years later, very little has changed, you should get chills too, when you read the rest in here. Which said again, IS ALL *Proven* Very TRUE!

This intersection, as I have insistently shared now several times, was out in the "burbs." This is what was and almost still is on the four corners, to this day. <u>1</u> corner-Mobil fuel station, <u>2</u>-Restaurant/ Pub, <u>3</u> adult bookstore a.k.a "Porno shop", and there <u>4</u> was a—quick fill, type gas station. NO sidewalks, No pedestrian crossing lights, No real reason for any normal person to **walk** in or around this normally very hectic crossing. Other buildings and house are all quite far back and even empty fields surround and wrap behind the corner lots, which all had a lot of high reeds and tall grass. Point being; who (in their right mind) would "take a stroll" on a Tuesday afternoon, anywhere near that area? I can't think of any reason or person that I would know who would do such a thing either, unless out of desperation. But to go out for a "stroll?" (wait!)

For the sake of clarity, this next bit of information, came to me and my wife, about a year after this horrific event. It was told to us by that man himself, who I thanked profusely for saving my life; which he so humbly claims not to have done. {Keep reading}; it gets deeply interesting and should evoke a great deal of introspection, at this juncture. We invited him and his wife over to our home. This was, about a year later. Because beforehand, I just wasn't physically and mentally ready for much 'till then, anyhow. His words to us, quite closely confirmed the police reports, and witnesses, that saw these events that took place, that afternoon, were absolutely frightful and enlightening, as well.

This man worked for the Church, right here in Milwaukee, he had true interest in needy people's well-being, and life improvements. I would say that in my opinion he is the finest example of a "Good Samaritan" gentleman that I would ever meet. Thank You again Sir.

"Just So Happens"

Almost immediately after the man rolled my body over and removed my (full-face) helmet, "it just so happened" that a "little old lady" came walking up and approached him, and asked if he knew C.P.R.?, Which he then just so happened after being quickly startled, said that he had been trained in the classes, but had never done it in a "real life" situation. **She *insisted*** on him then to begin blowing air into my disgustingly bloody foaming mouth, and she started to repeatedly push up and down on my chest. Shortly they got a pulse from me, and both looked a little relieved. Then it almost immediately dropped. They quickly began all over, until another pulse action was felt. It only lasted another moment or so, and stopped again, so they proceeded to re-initiate the C.P.R. action over a third time. My pulse lasted just a little longer, and they each breathed another sigh of relief again, until it suddenly halted, one more time. He told my wife and me that they looked at each other in total frustration and anxiety as to whether or not to keep trying. Then with a "should we try it one more time expression on each other's face?" They both silently nodded and repeated the exercise until the pulse was reacquired once again. After the fourth try. Did you notice something here? They didn't do a "three strikes and you out," or I really would be out. (hmm)

Oh and, Of course "it just so happened"—*please* . . . another woman who "just so happened" on her way home from her job that day, had gotten off the expressway one exit earlier and made a quick stop at the big grocery store a mile up the road. Interesting enough, she "just so happened" to have gone through that intersection on a left turn to go back to the expressway on the next ramp south. Yet again "It just so happened" she heard the crash, she looked in her mirror and saw a body flying through the air. And all of the commotion that it caused and it "just so happened" she was able to quickly stop her car which was now going in the opposite direction, and had to cut over a couple of lanes to get out of the other cars path. Then, when she finally could, it "just so happened" was able to get to the scene, as she came running over to my body, "just in time."

It "just so happened" Do you really only have the word "coincidence" to answer for all this. Please Then wait . . . "It just so happened" that she, was an I.C.U. nurse from the huge local trauma hospital that I would be spending the next month at. Oh ya, "it just so happened" that I was in her ward for the first few days as well, too. (hmmm).

Dear reader; are YOU, as a person, really just so, (let's say maybe) "cold" I'd call it; or say "shallow" of an individual, to not be able to give credence and respect to anything or anyone other than say "just coincidence?" Serious. I can't believe that someone reading this and now knowing the absolute validity of these statements via the police report, and the recorded witness testimonies, that one could be so critical in their own mind as to refuse to give the ability to at least some let's say "higher power" or maybe an {angelic interlude}, credit for that. In addition, try to picture that this "higher power" would "stoop" down to this little planet earth and have a personal involvement with a "dumb/ugly/short/fat low value motorcycle salesperson. Just think this thru. I know it doesn't make sense. But faith doesn't need to make sense to be true; just trusted.

When I asked, the gentleman telling my wife and I, of these additional details; remember he was the "savior" of mine, in this incident, he proclaimed to my wife and I, that this little old lady told him that she" just so happened" to be *out for a stroll*, exactly when the crash happened.; of course. Ya . . . Right. Who, other than anyone with their own "death wish" would be or even could be staggering, strolling, or jogging, around that intersection, with no sidewalks or even a decent place to stand. Oh this little old lady that said she was "just" walking by. She must have needed some gas, (no-walking) or maybe a pack of cigarettes, how about a quick snack, from the gas station. Or no, maybe she wanted to go the pub, (that wasn't open yet, because it had been closed down)-sorry. Nope, I got it; she must have planned on checking out the adult entertainment store . . . Ya Think? Ask yourself, 'Who is the one that really could have been there?" And yes, she was even "trained" in C.P.R as well. Some snide remarks, might say "yo mama" ha ha. Just try to get real "once" in your life, please for your own sake. OK?

Oh Ye of Little Faith

I do hope you are <u>not</u> one of those people that passively says "oh what a "coincidence," because there's too much of that sort of thing through-out this story; which is of course, again, I'll say it's all very true. Many living friends, acquaintances, and police reports (with "loads" of witnesses) to validate all of these comments. I'm saying this all again, just to emphasize the genuineness of this whole story.

115

"That" is, just like so many people that only give Jesus a "Ya, he was a good man, a good teacher, and maybe even one of those prophet, kind of people" beeeep . . . SORRY! Anyone who can fulfill so many, centuries-old prophecies, while he was alive; then so many more <u>after He died</u> (which he would supposedly Not even be able to control) as just a plain human; is only, "one of those prophets"? Please . . . How could somebody be so gullible to believe those kind of lies? Oh! Guess what. That means—You would have to "*Believe* Something" "but I thought you can't *believe. In* things you can't see or touch. Hmmmm Do you remember the old rock song from the '70's by Rush? "*Choosing <u>Not</u> to decide*, You Still Have Made a Choice."

I shared with you that I was taught how to preach and tell people about something that can't be seen or touched or recognized, it would be labeled as an *intangible*, like the wind or radio waves. But here now this story is just another physical proof (tangible) that it is REAL! And now living in this "wireless age, almost everything is "invisible." Now What? We "gotta" believe That Too? Oh my. Does your T.V. Remote really work, without wires? Is there string coming out of you cell phone connecting to another caller. OF Course NOT! Is there a singer or a band hiding inside your car radio? So don't tell me you will only believe what you can see.

He (Jesus) must have been "really *really*" good, to control where He was born & by whom (a virgin), then do all those miracles that hundreds NO thousands could attest to. Then, not have His legs broken on the cross, like they prophesied in the Old Testament book of Isaiah which said, "*His bones would <u>not</u> be broken.*" Did you know that when the Romans crucified, especially someone that might come down "'quickly" (less than a week) they would break their legs, so they couldn't push up and get more air. Jesus was already dead; right after He said "*<u>It is Finished</u>*". The Roman soldiers stuck a sword in His side. Oh ya, that's right he was buried in a rich man's grave too, (a very well to do Lazarus). You see, crucified "rebels of the Rome" almost <u>never</u> were set for a burial like that. And then there is a <u>non-biblical</u> Jewish historian named Josephus; who lived right then. He just wrote history as it took place in that day of the Roman Empire; not religious, At All! He validated many of these occurrences. In a court of law, you need **two** witnesses, 40 days after he was crucified, Jesus showed himself to over 500 people at on time. Can we then say that we're NOT going to believe all that?" So, is that your comment about all of this? Let's simply say "<u>it just so happened</u>" how's that for not needing any conviction in life that God IS very REAL!

Coincidence! . . . Still, . . . Really! "Ya—think So?" A little old lady "just walking by, who happens to know C.P.R., quite well; and an I.C.U. nurse, who "<u>just so happened</u>" to stop. I'll bet you guessed by now that I AM trying desperately make a very Clear, Obvious, Blatant, point here . . . NO?

The fella who was working in the little "quick fill" gas station that afternoon, called the crash in to 911, he too <u>"just so happened"</u>, six years later, got to do it all over again. YUP-no joke. Same person, (me again) same, bike, same intersection, same time, and then even the same direction. What would we do without the word coincidence? But more on that later. I told you that, "this gets good" Maybe even in a second book; yup, there is really another whole story after this one. Maybe some people just need more "proof". (Probably just a coincidence-ya right)

When the paramedics got there and rushed me off, to the big hospital five miles north of there, the two police departments, had to try to get traffic moving again. But with a car that had a 700 lb. motorcycle for a hood ornament, unable to be moved, stuck in the middle of the intersection; that alone became quite a challenge. I was told that it took two different tow trucks to pull the two apart so that they could be hauled away. My bike was taken back to the motorcycle shop, where it sat for almost a year, as pure totaled out salvage. But I won't use this as a Kawasaki "moment" type commercial. The bike was still in brand new perfect shape, except that the whole back half was "slightly-aha" crumpled to smithereens.

David Miles

I.C.U.
You don't see Me

Please remember, I am totally unconscious (but yes barely still breathing) laying in the emergency room, while a "host" of medical workers, like an armada, quietly scrambled around my body intent to see what needed to be done, next.

The word spread fast about the accident & maybe (permanent) death. Many people who weren't there, heard from my employees saw it right there, or a couple of them who were coming up from behind. But guess what (you won't believe this–but–there weren't any cell phones yet. Really! Can you believe it? So another one of the employees, rushed over to my house to tell my wife, what had just happened. And he would stay and watch our two young boys, so my wife could hurry to the hospital, to see me, and to really find out the condition that I was in.

After much shuffling and scrambling around my body, for over six hours that they kept me down in that emergency room. They then came gently and quietly and told my waiting wife in great disappointment, that I just wouldn't "make it" upstairs into the I.C.U. Unit. This was because I had been so severely. Injured. They didn't yet have a good idea of how much damage was done "inside." All my "vitals" were so weak, that they supposed internal damage was pervasive and severe. They just didn't know how much longer I would be able to "hold out." So the decision was made not to move me.

I don't know who finally decided that I was going to possibly still live, at least long enough to qualify for the ride "upstairs" to I.C.U. Then, very late into the night, they put me in the elevator and took me up. My wife came along, and after I was settled into a highly adjustable bed, and hooked up to oxygen and saline, they let her in to see me. A female medical person, or maybe a chaplain, came up to her, quite quietly and in a consoling voice, told her that she should not expect to have much hope, because "they were sure" by everything that they knew so far, that I just would "not make it"

118

through the night. So she should plan on just coming back tomorrow to pick up my belongings. Also, she should start to make funeral arrangements. As soon as possible.

It was a pretty exciting day so far, for me. There were many more of those still to come. That day, I was supposed to be participating in a Deacon/Elder meeting at the home of one of the other leaders of our church. When the call came to the fellas, that I wouldn't be attending, they quickly wrapped up the meeting and headed to the hospital, where they were told that I may be dead even before they arrive, or at least probably would be dead soon, if not by morning. They didn't even know, if I would still be alive when they finally got there, in about a half hour; so they hurried as quickly as they could. When they were called, my mom & dad also rushed there as soon as they could, and our old friend Hank, the owner of Oak Creek MotorSports, and some other friends, that had been alerted to my incident all made it there as quickly as they could, as well. Between crying and praying, everybody tried to console my wife, (after they had been given the details of the crash; no one had much hope), obviously, with little success. Many hours went by, now quite late into the night, they all gave their farewells and wishes, the room started to slowly empty out. My wife was offered a bed they would move into the room, if she wanted to stay with me through the night, but she had to get back home to our sons.

The next day, when Elsbeth was finally able to compose herself, she arrived at the hospital to pick up all my personal things, and sign all the "deceased" papers. But to her pleasant (I hope) amazement, and as strange as you might think. I was Still Alive! See this isn't a "ghostwriter" doing this book. (ha-ha) It's still ME! Please don't blame this "composition" on anyone else. Promise? Fine, then. My wife has since confided to me, that she even had been given "special peace" in her heart, that I would NOT die on this occasion. She said, That this peace gave her "real confidence," despite all the negative medical comments that had been hurtled at her, and she was still hearing, about the likely-hood of my death.

<u>Dead</u> wrong!

Despite the odds that my demise, would come soon, they did actually decide to take me down to surgery on the second day. Even though I was wearing a full face helmet, I had come down with such force, and I landed on my face, and ground the front of the helmet to look like it had just hit a power grinder; I landed so hard that I broke my jaw bone, on both sides of the pivot points in front of my ears. Then in the center of the very bottom of my jaw bone, where there is that great big "squarish" bone, I crushed that bone as well.

The lady surgical doctor that did the operation on my jaw, said she had never seen anybody ever break that strong heavy bone before but "lucky me," I did (weuu hew—another "first"). And sure enough, that's all I've done my entire life, is talk about motorcycles or God, and I have a broken jaw in three places. But now we know someone who did just that, "Kawi-Dave" the salesman or used to be huh? Funniest thing though, none of the medical people, either doctors or nurses, ever said anything about the status of my teeth, or any other parts of my body that might need some additional attention. (height, hairline, weight—nothing ha)

But even, to this day, I believe, in my heart, that the medical team had basically "written me off." I felt that pursuing further exams, would be quite fruitless. And, with that said, we know that they didn't bother giving me a "cat scan" or M.R.I. However, in the long end of things, I came out of the hospital-Alive. So further investigation on my part, even later, wasn't necessary. Or so I thought. I will say . . . Please take strong Note of This. They all did a "Great Job" in keeping me alive" And because of that I do Thank God, for each and every one of them. And YES I can still talk; and thank Jesus for keeping His word, on my healing.

Although, they kept telling my wife that I just couldn't be expected to go on living, "much longer." They did see that I had a dislocated thumb, and "road rash" like you just can't imagine. The one thing that they did share with my wife, was that my brain literally exploded inside my skull bone, like a blister that swells up, right inside of my head; so they kept monitoring my brain activity and movements. Which of course my friends have all told me later no one expected to see any brain movement now, since there wasn't any before. (Ha-ha! I'd bet Tom started that one-no?)

After a couple of days to their amazement, they moved me into another part of the I.C.U. They even started giving me some therapeutic exercises, like leg lifts, and arm moves, etc. (Your gonna love this later) I just kept eating and breathing through those tubes, that were stuffed down my nostrils, one into my stomach, and one into my lungs. They really couldn't do much more, because in my "comatose" condition, I wasn't expressing any issues, of pain, or agony; so they just didn't know of any other conflicts. I was told later that they were afraid to give me any type of pain medicine, or anything strong, that might conflict with the head injury or because they weren't exactly sure what kind of "unseen" issues there might be; do to my whole system; having convulsed and flailed through the air. (not with the greatest of ease, either). That became very important to me later, when I was re-evaluating all this, Please read on . . .

Then, after about 9 or 10 days in the I.C.U. they felt that I was progressing along amazingly enough to put me down one floor, then another with (less severe-cases). That turned into a big issue, too. You see, I was apparently making all kind of convulsive gestures, just trying to get out of the bed and back home. I also would make grins and nods when certain people came into my room, like the old friend of mine. Who helped us move to Michigan (yes Tom). But still, I constantly struggled to get out of the bed, so they kept me "strapped down" with Velcro ties around my ankles and wrists. Hank even thought that I must have fallen out of bed, one time, because of the bends and warps in my halo, and face wiring. (Hmm)

I got visitors every day, while my poor Elsbeth could do nothing but just sit there and wonder what was going to become of all this? She thought "How am I going to take care of him? Will he be able to live at home, or do we have to put him somewhere? (Kawasaki crate?) Some of the doctors told her after about a week or so, that I would probably never get out of a bed, or maybe just a wheelchair on my own. They also told her that they had no idea IF or When I might regain consciousness. They were trying hard to watch the steps of my comatose condition. I later learned and really wished that I never had to know, but now I do. When someone is in the state of being unconscious, they actually go through five steps or phases, before regaining full consciousness. But they felt that, there was little hope for much of a recovery, for me. Ya ya . . . some people still agree. {I know}

But they did keep putting me through all sorts of different types of therapeutic exercises, in the hospital bed. Then they even got me up and out of bed after a about another week and half. Then they had me doing squats, and leg lifts, and a little jumping, and throwing a ball; all sorts of bodily exercise movements, to help keep my muscles toned. (Just wait till you see where this goes.)

Chap. 12

"ROAD KILL!" Reality Strikes

I "instantly" opened my eyes, and just like so many scenes in dramatic movies, all I saw was dark brownish gray, walls. (prison cell?) They were ceramic blocks from floor to ceiling. I panicked and started to squirm as hard as I could, but I was so tightly restrained, at my wrists and ankles, which made me go into even more hysteria. "What is happening here?" Those straps were so tight that I couldn't really even move at all. It suddenly "dawned" on me, I was completely strapped down, "what's happening to me? (I felt like the Jekyll/Hyde character—strapped to the surgical table) Am I in a jail cell? Or worse?" (The Hardley plant?) I was truly, and frightfully, SCARED! Stricken with extreme fear, is probably the best way to describe my reaction. What did I do to deserve this? (I'm sorry Hardley) What's this all about? What's Going On?

Suddenly, I heard two little gentle, quiet feminine voices calling out. "Mr. Miles, Mr. Miles!" I strained my neck, to look down towards my feet. Then I tried to scream "Where Am I, What's Going On Here-Let Me Go?" "Mr. Miles you are in the hospital, You were in a terrible accident on you motorcycle. You were killed on the road, but then they gave you C.P.R. several times, and now your here, in the "best Trauma Hospital" in Milwaukee, they are really good at saving lives." (I get a commercial? yup I did get that business promotion) I must have somehow verbalized it, and said "Oh no the boss IS going, to kill me, if I wrecked that brand new bike."

"Don't worry" Came the reply, back at me; "about that, he knows all about your accident" came the other little female voice. "How can that be? I'm on my way to a deacon/elder meeting, let me go, I've got to get there. I've got to get home for supper first. We're having tacos tonight." (now this I can remember?)

"No, Mr. Miles that was two weeks ago!" "WHAT?" I yelped. They insisted. "What! That can't be, my wife just told me super will be ready when I get there, it will be quick, so I won't be late." "NO, Mr. Miles—really that was two whole weeks ago." "NO, NO" I just would not accept those comments. "It's True—It's true! Please settle down, please. Mr. Miles." Then they both, almost in turn, told me of the horrific crash I had been through, on the first of July, and they both gave me all the details, that they were aware of, including the fact that I had been in a coma for the last two weeks.

Two weak–Two weeks

I just simply couldn't accept any of that kind of talk, and continued to struggle. Sometime later, minutes or hours I just don't know, but later; my Elsbeth came walking in, with a great big grin on her face. She leaned over near my metal wrapped head, with all its hoses, and tubes. "Elsbeth! Elsbeth! What's going on?" I frightfully asked. "You were in a terribly bad accident, Dave. You were killed on the road, then resuscitated." "But what is today?" I pleaded. She look down to her wrist, then her watch, and said, It's Tuesday, Dave." "I know that, I know that, I've got to get to the meeting." "NO! Dave," she insisted "That was two weeks ago, Dave. All the men came to see you on that night" I shivered "What is today?" "I just told you it's Tuesday." "No, no, which Tuesday?" I begged. Momentarily looking down again she said "It's the fifteenth." "How can that BE?" I cried out.

She must have known that she would be the **only one,** that I would actually accept those words from, because she saw the resignation on my face, so she then began to explain in full detail what had all taken place, now half a month ago. Then I squirmed "What happened to Charyse's wedding? Did everything go Okay?" "Yes, Dave, the men took care of the whole wedding for you. It was a beautiful day, and there were hundreds of guests there, and everything went off well for you, Dave." She calmly said. Jeff and Charyse had a great wedding ceremony.

Who's "more dead?"

"Dave, you were coming home from work, and Kara and Al were at the intersection with you, when you were hit. The man who hit you was, the police said, "dead drunk". He was .20% on the breathalyser. He came up from behind you and hit you at around 50 miles an hour, and he apparently never even tried to slow down or stop, the police and witnesses said. Then you flew way up in the air and even did some somersaults I guess. And then you landed right back on his roof top. You went back up in the air, a little, and then came back down on his roof again, on your butt, and then you slid down and flew across the whole intersection, where you laid, face down, on your helmet. They said you were "lucky" that you didn't break your neck at the fall, because you went through the air standing up, like you were walking; and you were up so high in the air.

"Then a man came running over to you." She continued. "And rolled you on your back and took your helmet off. He then started to perform C.P.R. on you and then a nurse; who said she had just turned the corner, to go home, in Racine, kept you alive till the paramedics got oxygen on you and brought you right here to the hospital. The nurse said that she had heard the crash and saw a body flying through the air, in her rear-view mirror. And you'll never guess where she works, upstairs right here. She had you in her ward for over a week. She told us that when she saw you flying, she did all she could to pull over to get off the road, but the tumult was turning into such a congested mess. It took her awhile to get to you." but she made it in time to help keep you alive."

Elsbeth continued. "You were in the E. R. for a long time that night, because they were afraid to move you. When they finally got you {sort of stabilized,} they then actually did take you up into I.C.U. They had told me earlier, in the emergency room, that you most likely wouldn't live long enough to be put up there" "Where am I now?" I asked, her. "You're on the eighth floor, you have already been in 3 or 4 different rooms, so far.

"But, Dave you've been unconscious for two whole weeks already, they had no idea, if or when you might come back; to consciousness. Thank the Good LORD! You did! When I came up here this morning they told me, out at the front desk, and everyone was so happy, they couldn't wait to tell me, so I rushed into see for myself, and here you are, Alive and Awake!"

This next comment that I make, is only for the guys to read; because that's just how we "guys" are. "How bad is the bike?" I fearfully questioned. "It's junk, Dave." I moaned in shear disgust. "He stuck your bike over a foot and a half into the grill of his car, the police said." I asked her then "Have you been back down to the shop?" "Her reply was "No, Dave, I don't want to see that that thing, all mauled to pieces. Besides, I have to take care of the boys. "How are they doing, through all this?" I questioned. Tim is too young to really understand much, and Eric, seems to be taking it pretty good." Was her reply to that gut wrenching question? I loved those guys so much. I wanted nothing but the best for them.

"That drunk, never even slowed down even when he hit you, the policemen and all the witnesses said. Dave, they needed two different tow trucks to pull them apart. It was stuck into his car so far." My heart sank. "Hank told us, when we were up in I.C.U. on the second day. That they took it back to the store, and put it in a corner by the back wall." That did make my heart sink. It was brand new, I had hardly gotten to ride it. "Is Hank really mad at me?" I asked. "NO! No. He knows that you had nothing to do with it. You were totally innocent, in this whole thing. He knows you couldn't help it, and supposedly the guy has insurance to pay for the bike." she continued. "Whew" I felt somewhat relieved.

Friends to the End

A long time employee, who went to work for Hardley co. and had become a district manager over in Michigan, sent his wife over to help my Elsbeth take care of her and the boys. Scotty and Lisa are two of the "most incredibly" loving people that you will ever meet; and I'm saying this even though he works for Hardley co. ALERT! ALERT! This is **THE Finest** thing that anybody from Hardley co. had ever done, especially for me. Yes! See Scotty, & his wife Lisa started coming to the "young adult Bible study, that I had going on Friday nights, and they were friends with Randy and at that time his sweet girlfriend Carla. And those kids, became friends of ours (I know, I know . . . How could that be if he works at Hardley co.?) Before that he worked at Oak Creek MotorSports, with us, as a mechanic, and before that for a Suzuki dealer near his home. But after his own "incident" with a little old lady, in Milwaukee, he had gotten sorta "messed up" when she hit him. So he took a job with Hardley co. He and she, are two of the very most **awesome** & (giving) people. Who I appreciate them intensely to this day. That is what one would call a "true friend".(despite where he works-ha ha) Hiring Scotty, was probably the smartest move Hardley co. ever made.

While I kept nodding in and out of sleep, through-out the day, Elsbeth spent the whole time at the side of my bed. Now after learning of all these events over the last two weeks, the day had come down to a close, even after my mom & dad, and some other friends visited. They all had great big smiles on their faces, that much I do remember. It was probably the metal "halo" and all the hoses stuck in my "shnoz". (German slang for nose) Ewe.

Now, because I came back to consciousness, they no longer had the two little "candy-stripes" stay watching me. They did this to keep me from trying to tear myself out of my bed. See my friend / boss

Hank, was a very "adamant and insistent" type of an individual, who some would call churlish. When he saw what I was doing, (writhing) and all of the cavorting that I was going through. He and several other, of my visitors found that their suspicions were correct. I had actually fallen out of bed, few days earlier. They got so upset, they demanded the observers. Though I now was awake, they did still keep the hoses in, and I continued to have an oxygen mask over my nose and face as well. But the "weirdest" part was that catheter, oh man that was something else, I sure wasn't used to, when I woke up.

There was a very senior gentleman in the only other bed in that room that was next to me. He told me he had been there for prostate surgery and just before I went to sleep for the night, he was leaving. So now I'm in the room all by myself.

Right after he left the room, a very short 30-40 something, sweet smiling African-American gal, came into the room. She walked over to me and reiterated the story of what just happened to me and looked me straight in the eyes and said, "now there is only one thing you MUST do only ONE." With my expression, I must have shown my stupidity of what she was saying. "You MUST Forgive that man. Even if he doesn't want your forgiveness and certainly we know, he doesn't deserve it. But if you want to have {half a life}; you must." Then she wished me the best, and just quietly backed away from the side of my bed and left the room. She was one incredible person. She had told me that she was a Chaplain, there.

Chap. 13

O.B.E. or I.B.E.?

So. Do you think you are finally ready for this; Now? Here we go. My bed, in the second week of my hospital stay, wasn't set to lie flat, but the head part was slightly canted upward for my hoses to work better for my breathing. That meant that I could easily see who might come into the room, and where they were in the room.

Sometime, that evening, in the dimly lit room, the door quietly opened about half way, and a middle aged male figure dressed in typical medical garb, stood in the doorway, that he had just partially opened, while holding the door. He then began slowly moving in toward my side of the room, and closer to my bed. I instantly recognized him, like we had been an "old acquaintances," for years. But he was still holding the door, when He finally asked me, "How are you doing, Dave?" My immediate response to that person whom I knew was "You know." Nodding his head up and down he slowly stepped farther into room, almost up to the foot of my bed. "Yes, I do" he said "I just wanted to hear you say how you're doing" yourself. "I don't know." And I countered," from what I've been told, I'm almost in pieces, and not good for much of anything as a human anymore; and Elsbeth just said a short while ago, that the doctors told her not to expect too much, from my recovery. I may still be bed-ridden, or most likely at least in a chair for the rest of my life."

Moving ever so quietly maneuvered. He walked up and now standing, right at the foot-end of my bed with the two of us looking straight into each other's eyes. He began; "Dave, that Does Not have to be." he tried to gently assure me. "What do you mean?" I asked. "Dave, I want YOU to Want TO live." "Ya right." I snapped back, in disbelief.

Guess who . . . ?

Now this is where; if you're just not sure of what's going on yet, or who I am talking with, I can give you peace to the answer you might have wondered about. YES! The will to live is that Very *Very* crucial to the life sustaining of a human being. Read On.

You'll clearly see. "I don't want to put my family through all this. My wife and kids are going to have it hard enough, simply trying to take care of me. That's just not right. Why should I put them through all that grief, and cost? It's going to be hard enough for them to {just get by}" I continued. "Please just let me die and come to heaven? I, AM coming there . . . Right?" "YES . . . Dave You received me as your personal Savior back that night coming home, back from Lois's house, down in Chicago; you definitely are coming to Heaven, to be with Me; just please Not Now!" "You were taught that you have eternal security; and that's correct. Only after you put all of your trust, in my sacrifice for you." "When you believed that my blood washed your sins away; You were eternally saved."

"But why should they have to spend so much time, money and effort to try to take care of what's left of me; a blob, for the rest of my life?" "They Won't Have To Dave." He immediately interjected. I kept going on. "My wife doesn't deserve this. How is she going to make a living?" "She'll have you to support her and the boys, Dave." as he slightly turned his head he confided that, to me. "They said that they don't know if I will be able to come back, even past eighth-grade, in my mind." I added. (But maybe I never mentally got past eighth grade in the first place. Huh?) "That's Not True; Dave. You will."

This is where, I have to admit, that there are All kinds of "Proofs" coming out here, my fellow classmates at Concordia Milwaukee, could corroborate, quite quickly. Our school Dean/Religion professor who I talked about earlier made this point that I am about to expound on right now. Very quite outstanding at the time in his classroom; never to be thought of again, at least by me, until this instant. (1.) Knowing that I would not really accept who this was, speaking to me right now. Or what he had to say, unless he could prove to me a distinct Biblical proof.

That professor told us to "Never believe any person that tells you "The bible says . . ." Until You, go for yourself, and check it out; in context and definition, and application." So that's what I did.

So guess what the person speaking to me, knew that too, without my saying anything about that, and simply looked at me next and asked me this question. "What's the shortest verse in the Bible, Dave?" He queried me. "I instantly came back with {You Wept}."[John 11: 33] (See I did remember something) "Your right Dave, but why?" He told me things about myself that NO-ONE in the world would know, except my memory or conscience.

(Is it coming back to you NOW?) "Yes, but Why did I weep?" He inquired. "Oh please. I've now heard a hundred sermons on this section of the Bible; maybe you have too." "Because YOU had just lost your best friend Lazarus, that's why!" I almost chortled" "Dave! You are simply **wrong!**" "Again!" I thought to myself. Then He continued. "Dave, I brought him back to life, because I **had** to." "What? What do you mean, you Had To" I confusedly asked. "Dave, He would be with me in **Paradise** in a real short time, but I needed him **here** to be a testimony, and a witness of who and what I was and Am. Yes the power I have to deliver in resurrecting him was important, but I needed him here like I need you here. Why do you think I waited so long to come to Bethany, after I heard that he died?" "To prove beyond a shadow of a doubt that he was dead, and then they even buried him, in the sepulcher. Remember it says that he even began to {stink}." I gulped. "Now do you see THAT IS WHY!" "Oh," I quietly gasped, under my breath.

Isn't Three Enough?

"And That is why I **need you** to {want to, want to . . . Live!}" "Who cares how many Kawasaki's I sell?" as he shook his draped head back and forth, almost in disgust? I couldn't believe that I actually asked that myself (about Kawasaki's that is). "I need you at church." in a pleading voice, He cried out. "But why, we've got four pastors there now, without me, there's still three left; so why do you need me there too, isn't three enough?" I questioned. Then I "bemoaningly cried" "But I'm n SO MUCH PAIN!" "Dave, If I came walking into your church on a Sunday morning, who would accept me for being who I am, the **Savior of the World**?" he inquired." **No one,**" I responded quickly." "Why?" He instantly asked. "Because nobody would really know you, much less know that you are who you say you are." I postulated. "Exactly, That's WHY, I Need you there." He quickly snapped back.

I have to tell you now, that when He first walked in and we started our conversation, I didn't really expect to be able to believe that he was Jesus Christ. He clearly knew that, too, to He did tell me several things about my thoughts, actions and events in my life that NOBODY knows . . . accept my memory and my conscience. And now Him. That was proof enough for me, at that point.

"But I'm just really not that important, am I?" I fearfully wondered. Then I, began to deeply question all of my understanding that I had attained, when I thought that I had been saved by my total trust in what He had done for me, back on the expressway going back to Milwaukee, late that night in March of '72. "Won't I come to heaven when I die?" I hesitantly inquired, again (is that my disbelief talking?). "YES! Dave! As I just said before, You'll be with me, the Spirit and the Father in heaven forever, that's not at issue here, at all.

You know that you do have your "Eternal Security." You accepted me completely as your redeemer down at Lois's class that night. You have been completely <u>washed</u> in the blood that I shed for you. You *know that your sins are <u>gone (not just covered)</u>—As far as the East is from the West."*(Psalm 103: 12) "And *your sins and iniquities will I remember not any more"* (Hebrews 8: 12) He clearly "hammered that point back to me from all those years ago. "Dave; I just need you to be willing to want to live. *Please"* Now this is getting freaky, when God says please, to me. What else could I do? I've claimed for a long time now that I am a believer. So why not believe?

Sorry NO Refunds

My turn; I now say to you, please let me take another aside, again to further explain my crucial spiritual recognition of this whole conversation that He and I had just "now" exchanged. When I had come to the complete understanding of the absolute need of total acceptance of Christ as My Savior; with absolutely NO additions or enhancements on my part. No performance can have any value in removing sin, except His sacrificial payment on the cross. And again, clearly without regard to my "brand" of religion; I quickly came to understand that when I made this complete transformation in my belief, I had gained a guaranteed conditional fact of certainty as to spending my eternity in Heaven with God. Prior to that event of salvation in my life, I couldn't even imagine, such an absolute. But in the New Testament book of Ephesians in chapter 1 verses 13 & 14 *"In whom ye also trusted, after that ye heard the word of truth, the gospel (good news) of your salvation: in whom also <u>after</u> that ye believed, ye were sealed with the Holy Spirit of promise, 14. Which is the earnest of our inheritance until the redemption of the purchased possession, unto the praise of his glory."*

If you ever have, or want to buy a house, there is a condition that exists, that we Americans totally ignore in the rest of our lives. When you put a down-payment into place, it is called, *Earnest* money.

Which simply put, means "non-refundable" down payment; really you cannot get it back, for **Any** reason, at **All**! Period. That is what it means in the Greek too. When it says that *the Holy Spirit is the earnest of our inheritance*. "No Refunds. You ARE going to heaven! That's IT! Done Deal. Look I didn't write that, God did through the Apostle Paul's authorship.

Quick, would you like to sound really impressive to your friends? The Greek word for all of this is Theopneustos (God Breathed or inspired by God). Pretty cool huh? Just don't pronounce the (P) There I did lean at least something else at Concordia. "Theo=God, pneustos=breathed.

Yes, You can know for sure if you're going to heaven or Not. I had never, the intention of being able to prove my doctrinal convictions, but, Wow, Now I can. This is so crazy, but boy it doesn't get better than that. Not only to read it and believe it, but to be told right to your face, by God Himself; that those statements Are Absolutely Pure FACT! And True!

Now Stop Right There! I know some of you are going to "quite honestly say" "Hey that's just like **Fire Insurance** . . . isn't it? Yes and NO! Get real now with yourself for just a second.

Would or Could You or anyone, who had just been rescued from a burning building, or saved from drowning, or C.P.R.'d back to life on say . . . 27th and Rawson ave; even so much as "have the guts" to rob that person, or steal their car, or do them harm? I don't think so, but that is what it is like to being the person that wants to play the "Fire Insurance" game, with God, after you come to recognized that He has just rescued you from Eternal Damnation, due to the sins that You commit, in His eyes.

So Who Got Fleeced?

There was/ is a character in the Bible, who, was a believer in God; and he was even appointed by God to be a Judge of the nation of Israel. His name is Gideon. If you know the story, you'll know quickly what I'm getting to. If not let me expound. Gideon had real "trust" issues with God giving him directions. His actions would be quite paramount for the whole nation of Israel, but he just didn't want to take it by faith, (and there's a lot more coming about that soon), with the decision to following God. He kept putting God to "the test," as to the accuracy of his directive that Gideon was given.

Here's where it gets real "disgusting" to me, (now, about myself-that is). I pulled the same stupid stunt with Jesus, who was standing right there talking to me, face to face. Why can't I just completely trust him now? I said to him "If you want me to live, so bad, then put me back the way I was before this so called *accident*." He now stood directly at the side of my bed, and looked in my eyes and said "Yes Dave, I Will." "OK, then I Will regain the will to live." And He did keep his word. AMEN! (You'll soon, see)

Now tell me this, Who do I think I am, negotiating (anything) with God? As the world would say today, I must have, pretty (big ones) to do something like that. Or what kind of a gutsy idiot am I? That's probably more appropriate. In my case, anyway. Remember I told you I was left handed. Will that work for me this time; most likely not. If you ever saw me, you would have wondered why I didn't ask for more hair, or to be a little taller, or richer . . . No, at least a little leaner, hey? I just "caved in" and asked to be put back to "normal", which Elsbeth still questions if He ever really did. Ha . . . ha. (I hope)

Interesting as it may be, You must now know that within ten months, I was playing tennis, with my now four year old, at a local park, Okay, Yes He beat me, but I gave it, my all. And you don't even know how unbelievable that was—yet. Just wait, it's coming. A little more than a year later, I even took my wife on a big long motorcycle trip down the Smokey Mountains. It was a 1000 lb. Kawasaki (surprise) six cylinder touring bike. I did not have to strain, riding it, but I went through a lot of pain in my back anyhow. I really just needed to do IT, to find out, "how much was truly left" of me, in this body. Yes we had a great time, even though we didn't take the "Dragons Tale" route. Bummer.

So after I was assured that He would put me back to health and well-being, He. Assured me that the pain would eventually go away. I said "**Yes**" to Him. Then He smiled and backed away a bit. I blinked and He was just gone from my view; and the door did not re-open either. The weirdest thing was/is that I recognized and knew Him instantly, but no matter what, if you asked me five minutes later, up to today, I couldn't tell you what He looked like, except for medium age, size, and looks. I couldn't even tell you his type of nationality or ethnicity, be it Anglo-Saxon, African American, or Middle Eastern. I just know that he didn't present himself to me as an Asian/ Japanese person, because with my adoration for Kawasaki, I would have surely remembered "that one." He spoke in real good clear English too, not in Aramaic, like in the Bible.

Alright now Hardley folks, Yes I Am! A True Blue "All American" boy. I love this country as much as anybody you know. But I really respect the culture of the Japanese, who say "If we made it good today, we will make it better tomorrow." Not like I *was* so accustom to hearing around here; "if we made it good today, let's see how we might make it a little cheaper tomorrow." Yes I know, that wasn't how we all felt, but man, while I was a boy growing up on the very industrial south side of Milwaukee County, there was a lot of that. We used to get many customers from Kenosha, WI. Most either, themselves or some family member, or neighbor, worked at the *Rambler* Motors company. A new story seemed to come up weekly of the different *stunts* the employees, would pull on the company, like dropping a pliers or screw driver down the frame channel between the front and rear door, and after the customer who bought the new car would go over some railroad tracks or a big bump, they would hear a rattle/clunk next to them in the car. The dealer could never find the problem, until they cut the frame part away, and a hand tool would fall out. By the way R*ambler* isn't here anymore, and all those jobs aren't, either.

I've got to tell you, that when not doing homework, or in class, we "dormitory brats" at Concordia Milwaukee, would go down no more than a few blocks from the corner of the school campus, and sit on the sidewalk, next to the original Hardley factory and watch the men build the motors for the motorcycles. I don't know what they were saying, but they sure laughed a lot, when they were trying to line up the crank bearings and connecting rods. (we luv happy workers)

Back to the hospital scene. After my "unexpected visit, I honestly truly did "NOW" begin to have a "will to live," and I had *hope and confidence,* which just prior I had **None** of this. It became apparent even to the hospital personnel, those who would continue to examining me and asking me all kinds of questions, to see it I had any memory left, or where it dropped off or when. As disgusting as it might sound; I could remember many part numbers and vehicle specs from some Kawasaki's. (sorry) They told me that they noticed a difference in my "countenance" and attitude; and were quite surprised, because most people that have suffered something like "brain matter" exploding in the skull, usually don't have very good demeanor.

My wife and family and friends all could see that I was in a "quite good" state of mind. They were all impressed at all the Kawasaki specifications I could quote, but ironically I could not remember my best friend's first name. (shows ya how bad I was–huh?)

Chap. 14

Here we go . . . Again?

The next chapter in the life and death experience of Dave Miles, was my, trying so desperately to regain whatever was left of me, and to what ever level that I could be, in mind, body or emotions. I will say that I was going through emotional turmoil like I had never even imagined before. I would find myself going through extreme highs, and ultra extreme lows. Maybe I was "put through that" so I could *empathize* with folks who are like that naturally. In my "on-going" life now, I had gotten back into counseling folks. They were all very interested in my expounding on my recent life changing experiences.

I won't say that I was "suicidal, but close. I was in such extreme pain, and agony, that I could see only death as an alternative or release of all this misery.

Since "this incident" I, even to this day, I have very little "respect" for my own judgment on issues or things, be they large or small. I've lost confidence in my own decisions. Because it "haunts" me, that if I wasn't "smart enough," to somehow avoid getting "killed" on a bright hot summers day. How can I make any judgments that are worthwhile, appropriate or valid?

I questioned myself, over and over again. "Why didn't I see him? Why didn't I jump? Why didn't I just take off, quickly? Yes; you're right. I had few of those options. Even if I saw him coming, {and not slowing down}; where could I have gone? If I would have tried to "jump some direction, there was just nowhere to go. I had another cycle right next to me, and a multi-light traffic pole, almost immediately to my left. And going into cross traffic would itself been suicidal.

Leon's Frozen What?

God also gave me a "little taste of Heaven" besides my wonderful wife's desert making; it is called LEON's Frozen Custard. I didn't say ice cream, or pudding like-custard, rather the smoothest, creamiest frozen sweet flavored dish or cone of heavenly bliss, that's ever been created. (Okay just heavenly bliss then).

When I came to consciousness, and began to move around in my bed; somebody decided to get me up and out of the bed and try walking. So they gave me a walker, and escorted me down to a "gym" and had me doing some therapeutic exercises. Things like bending over, lifting light objects, turning, and even try carrying lighter weights. Then they had two female medical take me for short walks. Starting with the hallway on my floor, then outside close by around the building. As I progressed they even began to have me walk a little farther and longer. I always used a walker, with wheels in the front. They told my wife that I was progressing way beyond what they had ever expected me to come back to. (I hope she was encouraged)

One day when my mom and dad were visiting, I asked them if they had a couple of dollars that they could lend me. (their rates were usually pretty low) They must have thought that I was going to get them or Elsbeth or maybe the boys, a gift from the hospital gift Shoppe. So my mom reached into her purse and pulled out a few dollars. I had No idea where my wallet might have been either.

Then on our next, daily exercise walk, the two girls, who kept track of me, and reported on how I was doing even though I was walking with a cane, had me walking on my own.(whew whew!) They sort of let me lead in the walk on the public sidewalk, and just so happened that I didn't turn the corner at the big intersection, but kept crossing the street, sending "squeaky" screeches from both aids, trying to get me off the city crosswalk. They "dare-not" pull or tug on me, out of fear that I might fall or something. Their cries to return went unsuccessful, they were afraid to put a hold on me or jump in front of me, so they just kept crying out. "Mr. Miles come back, come back." I didn't, and they were forced to follow me across the street to this busy frozen custard stand, with me standing in my "outside" hospital garb, with just my "double bottom (open) hospital gown on. Cute huh?

This "stuff" is so good, that it is a "given", that when a U.S. President comes to Milwaukee. The whole entourage would go to "Leon's Frozen Custard Stand", which just so happened to be located across the street from the big hospital grounds, and on the same road as my "impact." Can you "smell" where this ulterior motive might be going now? Yup, that's where.

We did get across the street safely, and I walked up and stood in line and when I got to the window, the girl behind the counter, said "Hi Dave" how are you doing? You never would have guessed that I may have been there before. (I'm so simple) So then I motioned my head back and forth to include the hospital aids, and said I'd like to place an order. It must have been real "cute," me standing there in hospital outfit, with my big stainless steel "halo" on and brackets stuck into my head, and my jaw clamped shut, with another big stainless bracket and wires keeping my mouth closed.

"Sure, sure go ahead." she chirped, knowing what I meant. "I'll have a chocolate malt, and girls, what would you like?" They were both so scared and embarrassed thinking that they were going to get in trouble, and so I insisted "come on, order something. So the one girl chirped out with saying "a little vanilla cone please." I was clutching the money all this while, because those darn hospital gowns didn't have any pockets . . . but plenty of "air" space in the back hmmm. Somebody, since told me that I had a light bathrobe on, at least. So I put the cash, up on the counter and waited for our treats. See I couldn't order a cone or dish of anything, because I had this big stupid stainless-steel halo on and my mouth was still wired shut, so I could not eat now, except through a straw. So I excused myself for ordering a thick rich Leon's Frozen Custard chocolate Malt. (If you haven't ever had one, You don't know what your missing—come to Milwaukee just for that; it's worth it) Now don't think I'm some kind of frozen custard fanatic, just because in our big open living room there is a huge painting of a gorgeously lite evening at "Leon's Custard," painting it's hanging on our living room back wall. (That's a place that deserves it.)

Boy that was the most delicious frozen custard I had ever had. When we finally got back, both girls just blamed me. Boy that must just be the "salesman" in me, again. (go ahead and blame me on being a spoiled lefty.)

Oh . . . so Sweet

Most people that know me, have come to accept that I am on a "world quest" to discover and test each and every frozen custard stand that has now or ever emerged, since the days of the New York World's fair, when it was first introduced. In 1939—not 1964. Just to be clear. "Okay, 'Nuff said" I guess.

After the girls told them; everybody that worked at the hospital on my floor was taken aback by my "little stunt," but I guess they were really kind of impressed, that I took the initiative, and started to show some sign of being a normal (type) human again. Starting to display the condition of "thinking" on my own.p.s. See, I don't think my wife still has accepted that, to this day, or so she infers.

So the third weekend of July, they had Elsbeth take me home, just to see if, and how, I would adapt, to those surroundings again. It went alright, as I remember, but I must say that for the next many months, I couldn't do much of anything more than go from the bed to the couch, then later to the kitchen table chairs, and that was just about all. Boy, I really wanted to get "romantic" too, but I couldn't take that much pain, just then (ya—I said pain).

This may or may-not be the right time to tell you this, but I think that maybe this book should really be a {recipe, diet, quick fitness book.} OK, not really I guess, but hey maybe it could/should be? Probably not, but I have told you several times that I was eating through my nose. And I wasn't the skinniest kid on the block prior to this event. But I <u>did</u> lose <u>52</u> lbs. In just two weeks. So I have always planned on writing a "best seller" (ha ha), that would be called "the Dave Miles <u>Crash</u> diet" get it, huh? I'm sorry.

Along came August first (exactly one month later) I was finally allowed to leave the hospital and go home. Which I had been struggling to do from day one. When the time came, they got me a wheel chair, and put me in it. I got to the elevators, and down the 8 floors we went. When we got out of the elevator my Elsbeth was pushing me, so in the middle of the lobby, (looking for takers?) then closer to the front door. I suddenly realized that I had a whole entourage (I love that word) behind and now starting to surround me. There was something like 10-15 medical people all grouped and mulling around me, in the chair. What the heck? Then two of them, a nurse and a doctor approached me, while my wife left to go get the car. (I was hoping she would come back)

"couldn't be safer"

They said to me, "Dave, after talking to all the different police, fire, rescue,/paramedic/E.M.T people, about your accident. Just so you know; We will **Never** put this in writing, or give it to you in a deposition, or attest to it in any court. But we do <u>ALL</u> now <u>Know</u> that you **could <u>not</u>** have been in a better or safer condition or mode of transportation, to get "rear-ended" at that high rate of speed, than what you were on, you motorcycle. Your recovery is just phenomenal and so quick it actually seems sort of" miraculous". Seeing what you have all gone through. We wish you well and hope that you can enjoy the next say 10-12 years of your life. Because, after all that trauma to your body and especially to your head, and what it has gone through; that is honestly about all that we can expect you to live."

So was THAT some kind of an encouragement or judgment; when a car hits a stationary motorcycle? I didn't know how to take that. Remember . . . That IT, WAS <u>NOT</u> a Motorcycle accident. I sort of smiled through my stainless mouth brace, then thanked them for keeping me alive, and said good-bye.

The one doctor, continued. "Had you been in either a car or truck, with or without a seat-belt on, either the belt, steering wheel, steering column, then the dash and windshield, would have rendered you either as dead, or your whole front torso would have been so crushed, we wouldn't have been able to do anything, to save you." I again thanked him for his service keeping me alive.

When Elsbeth drove me home, and I finally got to spend time with my two wonderful sons who were, remember three & eight years old. We tried to get back to some form of normalcy, with me ya right. I didn't know how much of any of this they could grasp, but I tried to be like a good dad the best I could. My little guy, loved to come up and sit on my lap, and we would "horse around" making faces and things like that. I just couldn't do much more than that anyhow. If I dropped a fork or knife, it took all that I could do, just to bend down to pick it up and that was a huge accomplishment if I happened to be successful, that is. But the pain I felt in my back especially up higher, was then so horrendous. I hope no one reading this would ever have to experience the back pain that I felt, especially between my two shoulder blades. (No I don't have more than two.)

Elsbeth drove me down to the cycle shop a few weeks later, and I was greeted by the whole staff, I had a pretty good rapport with all the employees. They even took me in back to see the bike, Oh Man! was that awful. "Brand New" in the front, and "pure junk" in the back half. Wow. Yes, And I did live to come out of that. Just imagine. My cousin Ruth, then handed me a gift that they all knew I would enjoy and appreciate. It was a bright red Kawasaki (GPZ pit crew jacket). That Did warm my heart, a lot.

Now I don't know how I remembered, but one of the most important times in my life, each and every year, was getting to go to the Kawasaki dealer meetings. It was so important to me, and I brought it up to Hank, and Elsbeth, and my folks too. It didn't sit "well", with any of them, but after I got the "halo" removed that next week, I did everything in my power to convince them to let my wife and I go along with Hank, to San Diego, Ca. Even though I still had my mouth bracket attached.

California Dreamin'

Yes. It was very painful, but a spectacular time for me, and I got to see so many folks that I had known over all those years, including so many close and far away dealers and their spouses, and so many corporate folks as well. But the best part was getting to see all those new Kawasakis'. Don't take this wrong, but I really do like the looks and sound of a Hardley, I just don't care for the "uneducated type arrogance" that so many of them seem to come equipped with on the saddles. "Just get over it for once, not everybody likes the same thing." And please know that Kawasaki has had a manufacturing plant, right smack dab in the middle of the U.S. For at that time already 11 years. Now it's almost 40 years. Lincoln Nebraska, is the "Corn Husker" state, and the state with all those Kaw's. (Sorry Wisconsin, I just can't help it)

So as you see, I did get my way, maybe it was sympathy, maybe joy, maybe just cause I knew so many people from around the world now at Kawasaki, I'm just not sure, but we made the flight, and got to San Diego, CA, and I got to go to another one of my favorite things the New Model showing of 1987 Kawasaki motorcycles. A lot of the factory folks that knew me expressed their joy in seeing me and not having to come to Milwaukee for my funeral. (they could've come just for the frozen custard) But I was glad how it worked out too. We celebrated old times, and some wild crazy times around the world that took place on different Ichiban trips.

They always gave us a car rally to go on, and one time we had a rally in England, where everybody seems to drive on the "wrong" side of the road. Except two vice-presidents and their wives in a nice new Saab, that went head on into a farm truck who just wanted to stay in his left lane. (No one was hurt), Remember, if you ever go there just say "I'm passing, I'm passing, I'm passing" (and DON'T change lanes). Another time when going down the Autobahn with Hank, and another dealer couple Ted and Donna Nielsen, from a Chicago suburb, {Lake Villa} rode with us also. She and I were riding in the back seat, of a nice little OPEL Cadet, when Hank, who was driving, like he thought he was Mario Andretti, ground the whole left side of the car off on the median concrete wall, and guard rail, that was in the center; again no one hurt. Another time, we were walking down the cobble stone road, right on (I mean Right on) the Mediterranean in Monte Carlo; (awe, poor us) I was changing from a regular to a very nice expensive telephoto lens, (to see the ships afar off better.) Well old "klutz" dropped it, and it began rolling down hill, and almost into the "drink" many *many* feet down. But I caught it "just" in time. Everybody swelled up, then laughed. That was stimulating as well. All in all we had a lot of great laughs and good times to remember. After all it was at the Kawasaki's convention (*Let The Good Times Roll*)

Even at a later dealer show, a few years later; I pulled another" little" tee-a-tete. I knew the President of Kawasaki Heavy Industries (KHI) in Japan. They're the parent company of Kawasaki Motors Corp. U.S.A. His name is Hiroshi Noda. and he was at the dealer show. The first day there I met him in the lobby and asked if he and any other executive from Japan, would be willing to come up to my room sometime, to enjoy a real "special" treat. (you'll never guess) He hesitated and then looked at me and said, with a nod and a bow, Yes—Thank You.

The next day, his secretary told me when they would be free from meetings and could come up to visit our room. This is pre-"911." This was when flying restrictions weren't so tight, and I had brought a cooler filled with (yup) *Leons* frozen custard, and the special little sundae cups, the awesome hot fudge, and pecans, with the bottle of maraschino cherries, as well. I even wore one of those paper fold open boat style hats that said of course *LEONS* Frozen Custard.

We had a micro-wave in our room and I had a porter bring up the cooler with the custard that they kept for me in the hotel freezer. When they got to our room I was all ready; "so I thought", and I dished out and created a "Hot Fudge Peek." sundae for all of the eight, 7 were men and 1 extremely well dressed Japanese woman that said she too would like to enjoy one.

Only Mr. Noda, spoke English, (it was sure a lot better than my Japanese-which I don't speak) and he and the others were all dressed in very *very* nice business attire. They wanted to be careful not to get smooth creamy vanilla custard, hot fudge, or pecans on their outfits. They stood around chit-chatting in their home tongue, and of course I had no idea of what was being said. But I gave it my best. And I told them that I was trying to show my appreciation for all the wonderful things Kawasaki had done for me, over all the years. And that was why I was so *proud* to sell their products. They all ate, then left (after a bow) with great big smiles on their faces.) "Arigato!"

Danka

You see there is a premise here that I think it is now about time for me to disclose. And that is to any/everyone who believes in the God of the Bible, and his Son Jesus Christ. Even if you don't, this is a very valuable learning tool type lesson, to hang on to in life. Please, listen carefully to this. I don't think anyone, would disagree or dispute anything that I am about to say, but I really don't believe that the *serious* depth of its significance, is absorbed into one's life fully enough, until they acclimate it completely in their hearts.

That Is! To truly be "Thankful" at all times, places, and in all conditions, that we find ourselves in. Yes! That might sound "crazy" to some; but to read the Bible and pay close attention to that word,

You will come out of that learning lesson, with a great "handle" on experiencing the true joy of life. The story that you have been reading so far should exemplify what I am trying to say here. I was supposed to be "thankful"? Really come-on, now, get real, impossible, that's just not right. Are all of those thoughts and feelings going through your mind? Ya they did mine too.

For those of you who do think that I am nuts, let me explain. God is "sovereign," or in Latin, Omniscient, (All knowing), Omnipotent (All powerful), and Omnipresent (Everywhere at once). He put us all on this earth, for one great big reason. No, not just to see if we can "muddle or suffer" our way through, but to give us "free-wills" which had never been done before, i.e. God says "jump" the angels and any extra-terrestrial beings must say" Yes sir.—How High"-on the way up? There is no free will outside of this little planet.

So when an individual genuinely expresses from their inner being (heart) "Thank You God". It is just like a little tike, who jumps up on your knee, and expresses their appreciation to you for the toy, treat, time spent; whatever. That is why, months after the dealer meeting in San Diego, the U.S. Vice President called to tell me how "moved" they all were, and how NO Dealer had ever done anything like that before. They just couldn't believe it. P.S. These people were from the corporate headquarters, and in case you didn't know it, Kawasaki Heavy Industries is one of the largest companies in the world. {bullet train-tanker ships, airplanes-satellites}

In the book of Psalms 95: 2, and I Thessalonians 5: 18, you have two quick blatantly obvious examples of what I am trying to convey to you. It is the clear answer, and it works. You must admit, it works in your own life as well.

Psalm 95: 2 *"Let us come together with Thanksgiving, and make a joyful noise unto Him with psalms."*

I Thessalonians 5: 18 *"In everything give thanks: for this is the will of God, in Christ Jesus concerning you."*

Chap. 15

"The BIG Freeze" Worth Sweating Over

The "weirdest" thing in my everyday life, <u>after</u> the "accident", while trying to get through the month of August, which was one of the hottest months on record for us up here in southeast Wisconsin; and if you know anything about the upper–Midwest, when we get hot, we get really *humid* hot, too, ala Lake Michigan, Now get this, as hot and "sticky" humid as it was, I literally "froze to death" each and every day continuously, while I was perspiring from the heat and humidity I just simply could NOT get warm enough. I had on sweaters, sweatshirts, and heavy jackets, which really offered very little help. Pretty strange, you say to yourself.

Yes it was, and I could not get warmer, in any thing I did. Everyone said that it was "probably just because of the "accident" and medicines—I'll just have to "work through it". Speaking of medicines. I was very concerned months later as I thought about my *"special visit from Jesus"* in the hospital, with myself. I tried to almost "excuse" the whole thing by saying that it must have been the heavy drugs, or narcotics that made my mind came up with all of that. Doesn't that makes sense?

Then as I asked the different medical personnel that had taken care of me; they all told me the same thing. At that time, they never gave me any "pain medicine or narcotics. When someone is unconscious, they were afraid to induce me with much medication at all. So I could come out of the coma naturally. So the answer is NO! I didn't have any "hallucinogenic type drugs" 'or any other pain meds. that got me to see and hear what I did. The whole thing was YES! <u>VERY REAL</u>! Plus, I can tell you that I was in such a state of "la-la" otherwise, that I couldn't have conjured any of that up at the time; especially after having just woke up from a comma. As fall was coming on, I repeatedly had to cry out to my wife about the exasperating pain as well as the "chills" that pain was so severe that I had between my shoulder blades. It was very *very* difficult to walk, or sometimes just to sit and just breath. It was so intolerable to bend or lift, that I just sat there like a stone. Not wanting to alert the boys to any more of my problems.

So, she and I agreed, after some time went by that the New *Ibuprofen* pain medicine didn't seem to be helping me much at all. Even though I had been taking a 1200 mg prescription since they released me from the hospital. Out of desperation, I called the lady doctor who had released me from the hospital. And I begged her for any kind of relief. She told me on the phone to come into the hospital the next day and have some X-Rays taken. Then she would see what medicine she could prescribe. She explained that all those "muscles" that were pulled and twisted, from all of that flying through the air and turning and tumbling, it must have really up your back "muscles," she kept saying. And then she told me that she would try to find the right medicine to help that particular area, in my back.

Hurry <u>BACK!</u>

The following day, Elsbeth drove me back to the hospital and wheeled me up to the x-ray department, in a chair. They got me in right away and after they were all done, the radiologist came back into the room and looked down at me. He suddenly jolted to a stop, and looked at me again, and asked "aren't-aren't You The *D.O.A. <u>Who Made It.</u>*? I looked up and yellepd; "**The What?**" "Yes, Yes . . . that's

you! Oh, it is So *So* good to see you," looking down at my wrist tag
"Mr. Miles." How are you doing, now?" I shrugged my shoulders, in
pain, and smiled. He was overwhelmingly exuberant with so much
excitement to actually talk to me. Then he told me that they would
send the "new films" down to the doctor later, maybe tomorrow. I
said that I can't wait that long the pain was becoming so unbearably
severe, so they finally gave me the whole pack of my x-rays. He put
them on my lap and my wife {El} wheeled me back to the elevator,
all the way to the basement level where the doctor had her office
located. We got to her receptionist, and I told her of my plight, and
so she laid the x-rays on her desk, and said, "She'll (the doctor) get
back to you by this time next week." "What?" I cried out, I can't
wait that long, nothing is stopping or even lowering this exasperating
pain and agony. I need her to call me {right away} Pleeesee!" "OK,
OK" she grumbled and took the big x-ray pack away, while saying
"I'll tell her to call as soon as possible." "Thank You, Thank You."
I kept emphatically and gratefully repeating.

We exited back into the hall then, while we were waiting for the
elevator to take us back up to the lobby, to get to the car, a doctor
with some type of Middle East heritage, came up to the elevator
also. As he looked down at me, then at my wife, he suddenly stuck
out his index finger, pointing directly at me and loudly almost
seeming to announce; "That's You! You're the **D.O.A. *Who Made
It!*** Aren't you?" I, being quite taken back at the loud burst coming
at me sort of smiled and said. "Yup, That's Me, all right. As we got
on the elevator he was almost teeming with joy and excitement, to
be riding with us. He said "You are "MR. Miracle Man" Miles.
That's what we call you, too. No One at this hospital could believe
that you would live, much less, get released so soon. I am so glad to
see you again, Mr. Miles. Wait till I tell all the other doctors and
nurses." Somewhat bewildered, we left the elevator and headed for
the car, as he loudly wished us well, across the whole lobby. At that
point, with a brand new title, that I had just acquired, we quietly
went home, now waiting for the "ultra important" telephone call

from that female doctor that had released me from the hospital couple of weeks earlier.

I waited and waited each day and heard absolutely NOTHING from the hospital or the doctor. After the second day, I called her receptionist, again, and she told me that the doctor was out. (surprise?) So when she finally did call exactly **one week later**, here is what transpired. She said. "Hello Mr. Miles, this is Dr. *so and so* (we'll leave that one out), from St. Lou's Hospital." "Yes Dr. I remember when you released me from the hospital. Please tell me that you've got something to help me in this terrible, terrible back pain. That I am trying to live through." I answered.

Can you hear me now?

There was a long silent pause. But I could still hear her breathing into the telephone, in a sound of bewilderment and apprehensive confusion. Sternly she then began by asking me in a very terse voice. "Mr. Miles, have you been involved in another accident, since you left the hospital, last August?" I then in a bewildered screamed "A What?" She asked again "Were you in any kind of an accident, since you've been home?" "NO!" I viciously snapped. "Why would you ask something like that?" I then queried. "I go from the bed to the couch, and back to the bed, most times. It hurts so much even to sit at the kitchen table. It hurts terrible just to breath. I haven't gone anywhere except once, about a weeks ago, to the shop, that I work at. And then my wife drove me to the hospital last week for those X rays."

"Mr. Miles, I have some <u>very bad news</u> for you." in almost an attorney's litigation tone. "How can you give ME any more Bad news?" I nearly choked as I asked. She then said "You have broken vertebra in you back." "I What?" pleading again. "You have broken vertebra, and if you're not careful, the slightest little shift, could render you paralyzed from the neck down or your waist down. Actually it is two of you discs. T3 and T4 that have been crushed. All I could say was "You can't be serious. You mean that nobody knew that, all the while I was in the hospital?" The telephone then went literally, <u>dead</u> **silence,** with which that all was I heard.

Finally there came the "liability mandate requirements" "Don't you dare, bend over, pick-up, turn sideways, lift, do any physical activities like leaning, squatting, throwing walking up or down stairways . . . and on and on she went with the ordinances that I would have to obey, to keep from falling into a paralytic condition. "And if any bone would slip so much as a fraction of an inch, it could tear or sever nerves or tendons and cause you much greater harm." In a voice almost begging for mercy, I proclaimed that I had already done all of that unknowingly, since I was released from the hospital. And, besides, they had me doing that, **Right In the Hospital! During therapy sessions.** But she was determined to get this out to my hearing, so that I would know how imperative her demands were that I needed to follow. Of course, after she was all done; in a very "imperative" tone she demanded of me. "Do You Understand this NOW Mr. Miles?" I painfully cried out "Yes ma'am." But then, another long pause again, and she said, "well maybe you could be alright, since it has now been about 16 weeks since the accident." (Let me ask . . . Could anyone here "smell" a huge lawsuit coming from this?) Well I did <u>Not</u> pursue that route. I still wonder if I should have. Now you see why I had to change hospital name. But as tall and lanky as I was 5'6" and a half (not very) I am NOW a half in shorter even. I'm starting to shrink at 35 years old. (Come-on that's just not fair)

Later in another book (yes I had another very similar "coincidental-please") incident that you won't believe. It too is absolutely true. And you will quickly see why I had made the right move, in not pursuing them (the hospital), in any form of litigation. Yes . . . Yes . . . I had another extended time in their hospital. The chills have never gone away, even to this day, because all the nerve endings between my shoulder blades got so "messed up." {the e-mail address at the end will give you a "sneak peak"

I actually crushed two different disks, in my spinal column. Maybe now you see why I should have asked the Good Lord, to get "taller "too. This whole "thorn in the flesh" thing I mentioned earlier comes from the book of II Corinthians 12: 7-10 It didn't work for him (Apostle Paul-that is), so I figured I didn't even stand a *prayer.* (Like that, huh?)

Hello; Anybody there?

The dealership's insurance company, held the policy; because I was driving a dealership bike with a dealer plate on the bike, and yes I have a dealerships salesperson license. They demanded, that before any negotiations for all the medical and or other costs, that I had to get my own attorney, and that I should be required to see a psychologist, because of the severity of my injuries, especially to my head. By the way, my wife had been telling me that for years, too. So my darling wife would drive me once a week, for almost five months and as I sat and talked to the psychologist, he reminded me of so many concepts and conditions that I had learned earlier, back in my college days. Things like, when people go through major trauma, especially a serious head injury; they would either come back from that "brink of death" one of three typical ways.

1. extremely bitter, (mad at everyone and everything–unable to forgive–especially God)
2. extremely fearful, or scared (almost of their own shadow)
3. quite silly giddy or goofy, (trying to make everything a joke.)

Can Anybody guess which way I may have come back? Yes I did, Sorry. Kind of goofy. To this day, I thank the good Lord though, that I didn't come back fearful or bitter. Ya, I even think I'm sometimes really goofy, but life is so much better to live like that, than to be always mad bitter or scared. Maybe now is a good time for me to deliver my "Mantra" on life. It is something that I came up with after my incident, which simply says . . .

"LIFE IS TO SHORT—NOT TO HAVE FUN!"

I, do however "always" qualify those words, by saying "Only Good Clean Genuine Fun! Nobody gets hurt, or "put down." So that is how I've tried to get through all of these years, the best I can. Having fun doesn't have to be "bad-vulgar-vicious or anything harmful just plain fun or funny.

"Shrink"-a-dink

Back to the psychologist, now. He listened to me for hours and hours. He went all the way back, at least as far as he could in my childhood, and searched out how I felt growing up. I have shared a lot of my memories with you in the beginning, but my times spent at my Grandma's house and my two teenage aunts was very enjoyable too. My aunts Mary and Kathy, both were drummers in their High-School bands, and I sure enjoyed those things a lot. So guess what instrument I told you about in my life down in Chicago, was {come on—remember DRUMS} Yes; (Yerr Gooood.)

The Psychologist really was the first one that questioned me about my "motorcycle accident," back on July 1st. I didn't "go ballistic" but I got close. "Why" you might say, and I'd get just as upset with you; especially after hearing this whole story so far. You might think, that I'm getting "hooked" on semantics, but let me tell you, I do think that I deserve the right to be a "bit touchy" on this one, now. I'll explain that one in a bit also. Let's just see how good your memory is. Who was way past drunk? Me? Who rear ended who, at a very high speed, going right into a busy intersection not even trying to break? Me? Who violated any laws, just sitting still at a red light? Me? I think we'd all answer NO to that one. Now what was the violator driving (let's say an old {Ford} four door sedan)? What was the innocent victim driving? Well let's just call it the" most awesome" sport-touring bike made back then, that money could buy. OK? Please be kind, I can't help the commercial, I'm a salesperson.

Yes we were selling a German motorcycle then, too. But my ego just couldn't afford to enjoy one of those money eating "beauties." **B**ring **M**oney **W**ith ya"

Here is where I will ask for a "little slack" See as you now well know; I've been selling Kawasaki's, now it has been for 30 years. But all of the other "perks." I have put more miles on Kawasaki's then in a car, I now literally have "<u>LIVED & DIED</u>" on my Kawasaki's. So cut me a little slack, OKAY?

IT WAS NOT a MOTORCYCLE Accident! If you can't agree to that, please go back and read it again, or call Oak Creek, or Franklin, Wisconsin police departments, and ask for their records, of the whole incident. (they shared jurisdiction at that intersection)

The best part of all this, was when I had to talk to the insurance company's attorneys, if you're not in love with attorney's, you'll get a kick out of that part. And if you are an attorney watch out for enthusiasts like me.

So the psychologist, became very *very* careful how he worded his sentences and questions. I can blame that on Concordia professors, too. They were real "sticklers" on absolute accuracy and information. That's most likely why I am such a doctrinal fanatic.

Towards the end of our meetings together, the psychologist started to express his understanding of me, and how I seemed to have been doing, even after the severity of the head trauma that I had gone through. He was clearly sure that I was a very "unemotional" person. Primarily, because as he asked me about my youth and younger years, I could easily attain memories of events like vacations or family get-together, or other activities, but almost nothing about specifics, like extreme excitement, (except for the lighter in the backseat) or fear, or exorbitant foolishness. Again as he had reminded me of what I had learned, that a human being normally retains 85 % of what they do as a recollection because that occurrence is burned into one's memory by an emotion. My memories were quite "non descriptive" that it verified his observations He also noted that I had a clear *conscience,* because I had in all those meetings, expressed no bitterness, guilt, anger, regrets or remorse, or fear.(Must be because I'm a lefty-ya right)

I have to admit that I did enjoy meeting with him, which gave me a great opportunity to tell him of my encounter with the Messiah. He listened intently and conveyed his understanding of "para-normal" or "out of body type" experiences, with people that he had worked with and others that he had read about. He didn't dismiss it at all in any way shape or form. But as I told him of the validating facts that I was only privy to, in that hospital bed, and those things that no one but myself would have any knowledge of or about; He seemed to give it a lot of credence, what I all had to say about my deadly encounter.

The part that really made me feel "good," came months and months later, from the doctor that my mother was working for. He had "connections," and got a copy of all my medical records. (pre-hippa rules) Anyhow, the psychologists report came back saying that I had made a "complete 100 % recovery" (despite what my wife and friends might still think) ha-ha?

Chap. 16

Government In action . . . vs. Government inaction

In October of that first year, because of my serious <u>inability</u> to "move about," and the extreme back pain I was trying to live with. The fact that *this* accident had drawn so much attention. The Milwaukee County, District Attorney came to my house to have me give a deposition. I was never in the legal "field" so I didn't know what that was, back then, I thought I might be getting a (suppository-NO-enema?) yikes Because they were taking the drunk driver/almost killer" to court. (you'll love this one, oh . . . man—justice?) He assured me that they (Milwaukee County-judicial courts) would do "**All It could**" to see that there was "full justice" brought to this perpetrator. Now if I was a "vengeful" kind of person that would sound really good to me lying there in that condition, with that much pain. But that's just Not Me! I guess, I'm just too truly honest with myself. Realizing how much dumb, stupid and just wrong things, that I have done; that I just couldn't be that vengeful, knowing how easily I could have done harm, to someone. (not by driving drunk, though). I also know that he wasn't out to get me or anything either. At least, so I thought, anyhow.

He, (the guy who hit me), had his day in court, and the judge found him "guilty" on all counts, and set his sentencing date, for "Pearl Harbor Day" December 7th. My "gut" was right in this case though, I told my wife, that he would call me and be real nice to me, just before his court date. I was sure that he would be in hopes of some sympathy and lenience towards the judge, before his sentencing day. And sure enough about mid-November, I got the call. The most interesting part of that call, is that he never even once so much tried to apologize or in any way say that he was sorry. He just kept telling me how he needed his job, and to spend time with his wife and grand-kids. I sat and listened, but that was all I could do. The call didn't last more than a few minutes. Most people would call to express their remorse for what had happened, so they could try to clear their conscience, a little, at least. But nothing like that came from him, that day.

Three hots and a cot

As I was told by some security officials who worked in the local prison system awhile later, He was given two full years, because I did come back to life; otherwise it would have been five years of incarceration. But this is where justice doesn't seem to be too fair, sometimes. Alright, the judge sentenced him to two years, but then he reduced it to only 18 months more, because he had already served some time. Besides that, all the holidays were "right around the corner" the judge said that he didn't have to report to the Huber Law jail, until January second, so he could spend the Holidays with his family. By the way "Huber Law" in Wisconsin, means that you get to leave the jail every day to go to work; just come back after work, have a nice supper and go to a nice warm and somewhat comfortable bed.

He drove eight miles from his house and he reported in on January second the day he was supposed to. They looked through all of their records and couldn't find his name listed anywhere. So they wouldn't accept him as a prisoner, reporting to start his sentence. It just so happened that this gentleman was a 54 year old, who was seemingly quite healthy, fella. They told him "No, {three hots & a cot} for you pal. Get out of here" So he left.

Either he was feeling a little guilty, or just downright smart, knowing that the system would eventually "catch up" to him, after the "red tape" would finally come through, he went again the next day; still not on the list. When he gave it a third try, sure enough his name the "popped" right up.\

So, the prison system *apparently* felt that they had "screwed up" so bad, by not letting him serve his appointed time. The county court system, released him after serving a whole nine months, and he was a free man, again. Should I be bitter? I think that it would be rather expected of me, I guess.

Do you like "bitter-root?"

This is where I must share with you what I had learned in my college Psychology courses and then was re-freshet in my memory by the psychologist. "Everybody has valid reasons for being bitter, for one cause or another, maybe it was their upbringing, or a family member, possibly a spouse, a friend, or bad job, or maybe No job at all. It just doesn't matter what the cause is. (a lot of people are bitter towards God–if He really exists; is their question) and because of the issues in their life, that He could have changed. Guess what? Only the person who is bitter, feels that pain, and the other party may not even be aware of your issue with them. Because "items" in your life don't just go "heavenly" you think you have the right to blame (be bitter toward) God? If you think that YOU or ME, has the Right to be bitter. Just read the Old Testament book of Job. (not job-like work-but Job, sounds like globe). He had EVERYTHING!—Yes Everything taken away. Guess how He handled that?

Truth is; I simply refused to be held in my own personal incarceration by "things that didn't go well". Why should I let that kind of feeling control me, for life? Nothing is going to change any of it now; the past is past. Let me ask. Would any one of you reading this book, deny me the right to BE bitter? Then tell me what good would that do anybody if I was? See, why should I, or anyone else with the right to be bitter, just *rot* in that terrible stench of anguish? We all like to have wishes and dreams that things are going to get better; and they usually do, but the smart move would be to "hang in there" till after that last breath. Only so, providing that you DO accept the Savior who forgives Your Sins, to qualify you to get to Heaven. See, God never promised anyone "Heaven on Earth!"

Have you ever gone to a concert, or ball game, or maybe some large event. "Scalpers," <u>won't be,</u> at the Gates of Heaven, but when you try to get in to any of those arenas in life, if you don't have a ticket, or pass, **You Won't Be Let In**.! **Period.** It's as pure and simple as That. (remember 3 Dog Night?) I'm really not trying to preach here (even though I am ordained, and not through the internet), but please live your life to the fullest. You just don't know how much time you've got left. None of us do, so why waste it? Think of it like this Once the game is started Nobody else gets in. Period! (Last breath) **<u>GAME OVER!</u>**

Why do so many people seems to try to "race to the grave?" by something so simple as NOT wearing a helmet, while being on a cycle? Makes no sense to me either.

Recovery did take a long time; that's pretty understandable I guess. The doctors told my wife and me, that how I was, after 18 months, my recovery would hold at the total extent of my healing. I just couldn't wait that long, so I pushed myself as hard as I could. After I left the hospital, I got, No other (sanctioned) therapy, like there would be now-days. I knew that I had to do something to regain strength, so I tried getting back into the "fatherly" home-school side of things, with my boys. Doing little projects at the kitchen table, then down in the basement on the work bench, when I could finally go up and down the stairs. We would make little things like bird houses. My youngest little guy and I even made a patio chaise. Just to learn how to "do things" with tools. I kept assuring him that I really wasn't the carpenter or mechanic to show him the "professional" way to do things, but just to give him an idea, what those tools were for.

I will admit that I did come out of this with a few variations of "thorn in the flesh" issues, or life lasting after affects. Because of the way my brain "exploded" inside my skull, that messed a few things up inside (surprised), how I lost a little part of my vision. Say you're looking at an "old fashioned" circular clock. In the middle where the hands mount, if you looked straight up to the 12, I have no sight between there and the number 1. Only guys are going to understand this next comment. Because I broke my jaw bone, down on the bottom, when I shave down at the bottom of my face, the pain and overspreading hurt on my neck and chin are just simply horrible. (nerve endings again) The worst part is that I can't grow a beard, because, now no hair will grow "right there". So having an odd shaped hole on the lower right hand side of my cheek, really looks stupid. Oh well "poor me". Ya-Right.

The Tooth Fairy, Never Showed

The real interesting thing was how, while in the hospital and even after I left, I never was told about my teeth. However all the medical people kept telling me to make an appointment with my dentist, for a "check over" So when we got home, a few days later they got me right in.

The first thing that I said to the doctor, "was please take these ridiculous slider plates off of all four of my molar sets." So he looked inside, all around and pulled his mirror out and stood up and asked "What slider plates, Dave?" I opened my mouth again and showed him by sliding my tongue back and forth, on those "stupid" sliders, then I used my finger, and said "see." "Dave, there is nothing in your mouth but teeth, he looked again and felt around with his tool. Then he stood upright, raised the chair up to see me better, and said "Dave, I'm not sure how to tell you this, but all of you molars have broken off of their roots, and are sliding back and forth on the root stumps of you teeth. I tried to scream "WHAT!" He nodded and said that he would have to put crowns on all of them. I didn't have dental insurance. He said that wouldn't be a problem, because they too, knew all about my accident, and that they thought they could get the insurance to cover that from the accident, as "facial reconstruction." My wife said that It didn't help my looks, one bit. Bummer; and let me tell you, I wasn't good looking to begin with.

18 hours over almost three months of visits, sitting in his chair for all of that "excruciating" grinding, chipping, digging, and then replacing of my teeth. All you could hear was his drill and I could hear, smell, and feel chips of seared teeth splattering out of my mouth. While just sitting there in pain, I got so mad at my mother. She always scolded me for eating too much candy and ice-cream, because I would ruin my teeth. So now what; just think of how much more of those enjoyable goodies I could have relished anyhow. ha-ha

Chap. 17

Having Fun with Insurance

B ut this is where it started to get sort of "fun," at least for me. The dealership's insurance company was on the line for a lot of money, since the fella who hit me, had minimum state law insurance $25-50&10 K. I was told that they paid up in ten days. Problem was even in 1986 my initial bills went way over $ ¾ million, Hospital, Doctors, Radiologists, Emergency personnel, etc. on the road and in the hospital. It really all adds up quick, but I was in there for a month too. And with all of the one-on-one care, it cost. So the insurance company was really busy, behind all the scenes. It wasn't just because I was on a company bike, but I had a lot of different company papers along, in the saddlebags, because the next morning before I went to the store, I was going to work on those papers. (should we say home office?) I guess that because I was a company officer as well (vice-president) it had a lot of impact too. I only had to shovel the dog "pooh" once a day, and clean the bathrooms once a week.

My attorney called me and said that we had to go downtown to another attorney's office, for a deposition, (now I knew what it was). One day early in spring of 1987, he picked me up and drove me downtown. We went into this attorney's office, then into a conference room, where my attorney sat at my side and three very "studious" well dressed gentlemen sat down across from us at this long conference table. They introduced themselves and put the tape recorder out on the table and turned it on, then began by announcing that this meeting was being recorded and did I know that. "Yes I know." I said, and they started their questioning. This is where I finally got a chance to have a piece of my mind, expressed. "Today is February 17th 1987 and we are here talking to Mr. David L. Miles. "Good morning Mr. Miles" They began.

"Good morning gentlemen." I smiled and quietly chirped back in my reply. "Mr. Miles, We're here today to talk to you about your motorcycle accident of July, 1st 1986, Please tell us what you remember?" Was their first request. "I looked the one attorney in the eye, and smiled to say. "What motorcycle accident?" My attorney even jolted. Don't you remember anything about that horrific motorcycle accident that took place with you, on 27th & Rawson ave. last July 1st?" I grinned and said "Nope" With a jerked reaction, by pulling their heads back, the insurance companies attorney and cohort, looked at each other in dismay. My attorney whispered, Dave what's going on. I sat still and ignored him. Then one of the other attorneys looked at me again and asked. "Mr. Miles, is there anything that you do remember and can tell us about last July 1st?" Calmly, distinctly, effortlessly, I began, by saying that I got up, spent time with my little boys and wife, had breakfast and went to the store. It was very hot and sunny, and we had a lot of customers, early in the day. Then he interjected, "No, no Mr. Miles, do you remember anything about your travels home after work that afternoon?" "No" I quickly snapped. "I only remember saying good night to Kara, Al and the other employees, as I locked the door."

What motorcycle accident?

"Mr. Miles, Did you know that you were in a terrible horrific motorcycle accident, while driving north on 27th St. in the left hand lane. "Nope" I returned. "You have NO memory of the motorcycle accident that initially took your life?" "I said, "No I don't remember it At All!" "Has anyone told you, what had happened that afternoon?"

"OH, yes of course, a lot of people have told me about it, including a lot of the police who were right there after it happened. I know most of them personally."

I was told that he "rear-ended" me, while I sat there, at the RED light in the left hand lane, I was totally stopped, and then there was a motorcyclist, whom I apparently saw coming from behind in my cycle mirror, just prior to all that. And I was then told that I moved over to the left hand side of the left hand lane, so that he could join me in that line at the front of the light." "Have I got all this right, so far?" I asked them. "Yes, yes . . . go on Mr. Miles." "I was told that on that bright hot sunny afternoon, just after 6 o'clock that "aforementioned" car came "steaming" up behind me at speeds of almost 50 miles an hour, and obviously had no intention of slowing down or stopping, since there were **No** tire screeches, or any fresh tire tread marks left on the road. The car hit the bike that I was seated on, just sitting there and waiting for the light to turn green, and it stuck the cycle over a foot into the front end of his car, and into his radiator." "What happened to you Mr. Miles?" They queried. "They told me that I went flying way up in the air, then after 2 reverse somersaults when I came down, feet first, I crushed in the roof of that car that had just hit me; right over the drivers head. Then I landed again on the roof, with my butt, then slid down the windshield and flew in a standing up position almost all the way across the whole intersection.

Everybody was amazed that I didn't hit any other vehicles going across, but they thought that I was still high enough." "Go one please." was their next request. "Well what they told me was that the guy **never** put on his brakes, but my motorcycle actually stopped him." They said that he almost got me *again* with my own bike, a second time." When his car finally stopped, he lurched out the driver's door, and began apologizing that he was blocking traffic, because his car had stalled. The people started scrambling all around and hollering to him that he hit someone and they are laying "over there" dead.

The police got there quickly, and arrested him, and put him in one of the back seats of the two different police departments' squads. He immediately "passed out" on the seat, after regurgitating several times.

"I came down on my chest, and slid a good ways and ground the whole front of my full face helmet into the asphalt. A fella, who was now stopped by the whole collision, came running over to my motionless body, and rolled me over, then he took my helmet off, and saw lots of blood spewing out of my mouth. Have I still got this right, so far?" I asked. "Yes, Mr. Miles that is quite close to how the two police reports described it as well."

"So Mr. Miles; How can you dare say that you were not in a motorcycle accident?" As they squirmed in their very nice "button down" leather seats, waiting for my response. "My question to you gentlemen is then HOW Can You Call this a MOTORCYCLE Accident? Who had the accident?"

"Gentlemen there's only one major problem that I have found with your questions today. If this gets somehow listed in the official government and insurance records as a motorcycle accident, I will have my attorney here, sue the liven' "be jabbers" (what kind of word is that?) out of Your attorney's firm, for completely and totally misrepresenting the truth." "WHAT?" Came back as almost a screech. I started back in, right away. "Have I not been told correctly, that a man in a dark red older Ford four door sedan, was in a drunken stupor, and being in a "dead drunk" condition with a .20 blood alcohol level, rear ended me, on my almost brand new motorcycle, which was totally stopped at the red light? Everything came to a precise halt. Both of their "inquisitor" heads turned toward each other in bewilderment, and the one attorney, turned back and asked if "could we have a twenty minute recess?" My attorney nodded yes. I must confess. I just sat there for the next twenty minutes *gloating*. Gloating. Like a Kaw? Not a pig; that's for sure. (I know; it was a very prideful moment—sorry)

When they came back; I must say (seemingly rather sheepish) they sat down and asked both of us. "How about if "we" label this accident as a "pedestrian-style" incident for the state and insurance records. Would that be acceptable Mr. Miles?" I sat and pondered and then turned to my attorney grinning and him and I both agreed that we could "live with" that for a title of the accident. Inwardly I squealed with delight.

It's all just "semantics"; again, you might say. Maybe that is how you'll feel about it, but someone like me who has devoted almost his entire adult career in the motorcycle business, sees these type of miss-statements as such a miscarriage of information. I take alert. Remember what I shared earlier, when I was exiting the hospital, even the medical industry saw the strong inappropriateness of that kind of damning announcement. I couldn't have been on or in a safer mode of transpiration.

This is "kinda" hard for me to say, but I always try to be forthright and honest. NOBODY in the world has what Hardley has! No I don't mean in the "Asian" quality permeating their bikes, but rather. In the camaraderie. It is so true, if you call a few friends to go for a ride, in less than 10 minutes you've got 6–12 guys ready to go along with you. That is really a Great Feeling. Congrats. Hardley. And don't forget to thank President Reagan for all the free publicity he gave you with "Buy American, Made in the USA, back in the '80's Which of course we now know is a bunch of bunk. But hey it still works for ya. Run with it. It simply doesn't matter, who makes a more "exact" look alike, if the emblem doesn't say Hardley it isn't the same ride. Period. Again "Good Job"

Just keep a "lid" on it

Just please take note, and remember what I have been saying all along, that I was wearing a "full face" helmet. (Not just to keep from scaring little kids along the road), but because, as we've all heard is true "It's Better to Be Safe than Sorry" Why be an idiot and think your "so cool" you wouldn't wear one of those "darn" things. Their too hot, and not comfortable. And "I'm careful." Think that a handkerchief "dew rag" tied around your head work as well?

Let me say this: If I didn't have a full face helmet on, there just simply, wouldn't have been enough face to C.P.R., so try to convince me otherwise. Just think of what that poor medical angel and fella must have had to look at when they successfully endeavored to save my life. It "ain't" pretty, even without the blood You might be another one of the "coolest" people in the cemetery. (underground that is—not visiting) Why "Race to the Grave"

But this is where I will get on my "soap box", please allow me a few words to interject my personal opinion (now–quite qualified). Squeeze the most "Joy and happiness" out of life that you can. If you *want to be miserable* **don't believe** what **God** tells us in the Bible, about the_need to receive His Son Jesus as Your own personal Savior. If that is your choice, you'll have a whole eternity to really be miserable. So why start now?

If you are one who says, "I can't believe anything that I can't see." Boy are You lying to yourself. Your whole life is nothing but "TRUST." Is there really Gold in Fort Knox? Will the president really "stand-by" the constitution, Will my "special one," really stick with me, Will this paycheck really be good, when I get to the bank. (ask the folks in Cyprus), Will this "stupid" red light ever change?" Will my run in the Boston Marathon be safe? Will my Daddy win, so I can run over to congratulate him? Even though I'm only eight years old? Did you catch that? They are ALL trust issues. You've gotta trust in "something"; else you couldn't even breath. Tell me can you see your lungs work, or your heart beat.

As seen by some as corny. Wearing a helmet, and protective clothing, making sure all your lights and indicators are working, can all have an impact (or prevent one) but, hey, that isn't always going to be enough. Just ask me again. But, what if I had been say, walking across that intersection (probably helping that little old lady get to that bar, or porno-shop-ya right) by the lights and got hit by a car that didn't so much as slow down, you can be assured that I wouldn't have had a helmet on, and would be dead on the road, just the same.

Guess what? After what you have just read. I would Now be in Heaven. Not because I deserve it, but because of what Jesus has done for me (& you). Only difference is that I have accepted that promise. (Will you—Have You?)

We all know how so many vehicle accidents are caused by alcoholic input. Tot alcohol itself, but the "improper" consumption. Now I'm not against alcohol either. But let's face it, self-discipline is what is the big need here, in life. You can only take control of what YOU do with your own life and discipline is the first starting point.

Now comes the ministerial teaching part of this book. (Ya . . . I know; close the book and go to bed. Or maybe you'll learn something, and besides, it's almost done. Okay? One of the most interesting things that I learned at Concordia, was that the VERY First SIN, committed in the Universe, was PRIDE! Not eating of a piece of fruit. "Whoa!" You might say, I may not go to church much, but I know it was the "Adam's apple". No, be you Jew, Gentile, & or Muslim, all are supposed to abide by the information given in the "Old Testament of the Christian Bible, Hebrew Bible (Pentateuch-Torah), and the Qur'an."

In the book of Isaiah 14:12, the story of Lucifer (Morning Star, Shining One) is explained. It has a lot of similarity in the Qur'an. He was the highest created angel, and he decided that he was going to be "as God". Now that's guts.(Please take it from one who acts like he has'em; I didn't say brains) God did not stand for that one long, at all (surprise), and cast him and 1/3 of Heaven's angels that followed him {Lucifer}, down to utter-darkness and destruction, but first to this earth (right here).

Would we all agree, that those kind of words would simply come from a strong act of PRIDE, or Arrogance? I think that would be a good definition. It's Not pride in your country, or pride in your hometown team, or pride in you work. But when that "bugger" gets real personal and controlling, is when all the trouble starts. So many people, be they bikers or not, let their "pride" have control and then they see themselves as "invincible". And if your honest with yourself, you'll agree, that doesn't usually last too long, or genuinely get you to far, either.

Any psychologist will tell you that we all "need something to hang on to," to help get us through this life. Pride is a common entity that many of us grab on to. But when that is challenged or defaced, we get crushed, and scramble for something/someone else. Just look at the divorce rate to validate that.

The example you read back some chapters ago, when we at Oak Creek MotorSports became the Nations Largest Kawasaki dealer", I was so "YES" *proud*. Hank, was in total ecstasy. I hesitantly told him one day a few months after our award, "We've only got one direction that we can go to, from here." He almost reached out to strangle me for having said that. It's not a good feeling; it's just pure truth, and simple reality. Why do we want to always run away from *truth*? We want to cling to the pride full hold. Ask any car dealer, they'll tell you "It's all in the attitude of "How Good You are"; I ask you to please don't think that I'm *Against* pride; I'm Not. Just don't let it "run your show."

I am very proud of Kawasaki Motorcycles that I sold, yet I own other vehicles as well. I was raised by my grandpa, and parents to be proud of the *Chevy's* we all drove. Then I went out and bought a Ford Torino, (station wagon no less).ewe. How dare I do something like that? Pride can be a big influence especially in relationships, but as I keep saying, don't let it control you. It's JUST NOT Worth IT!

I haven't said anything, so far about my "personal life" growing up. {you haven't, you say—what's this all been) No; but wait. Being conservative must be in my genes, because before we had moved out to the lake (I was about two and a half). Easter of '53; my parents gave me some Easter eggs, and candy. Now I was pretty small so I don't remember all the details, but I clearly remember a few weeks later, that my parents started searching the apartment for a dead mouse-maybe. It started to stink up in that apartment; really *really* bad.

We are now getting into very warm weather, and both started to realize that the smell was worst in my little bedroom, and so my dad started searching all around, in heat vents, and closets, when he got closer to my wooden toy box the stench got stronger, so he started to carefully pull all my "little kid" toys out. And when he got to my little brightly colored metal lunch-box and opened the lid, I was just standing in the doorway, he literally fell backwards, and almost passed out from the disgustingly, ghastly smell of the two "pre-shelled" rotten Easter eggs, that I was "saving" for later in there. Oh well, am I, too conservative?

As a three year old, One day at Grandma's house, in late summer. I sold two bags of apples that my grandma had put out, on the sidewalk in front of her house. My mom and she were sitting on the porch watching me, when an older woman walked by and asked how much a bag of apples would be. I said a dime please. She said "I'll take two bags", and handed me a quarter. I "freaked" and ran back to grandma. I didn't know what to do. She said "That's a quarter" and the women gets a nickel back. So I ran back to give her the change she was due. She told me to keep it, all, as she picked up the bags and walked on. Maybe that's where I got this "salesman" thing going". Yes, then I was so *proud,* and I sure liked the sound of profit.

For many years, as I was growing up, (ya it took many years–for me) I would go spend some time with my mother's parents. My grandpa, was a milk-man; not the kind that brings the milk to your door, but the guy in the big truck that went to the farm and got it from the cows (not the Kaws). Now in a great big stainless steel tank, in a special milk-house. I learned how to milk cows, feed chickens, plant corn and all the things a farmer has to do. (let me tell you . . . it is A Lot . . . too). Then after the truck was full and all the farms had given us their milk, we would head back "into town" and go to the dairy plant to drop off all the milk that we had just picked up. That was fascinating, watching all the activity and "super clean stainless-steel equipment all around. It was the old original Borden's dairy. (And you know that they were all Kaw's? Cow's—oh well) Is that why so many Hardley people are "lactose intolerant?"-Hmm-new revelation. They have such a hard time with Kaw's milk.

I also worked at a huge Milwaukee county Park for two years in my high-school days, (before Oak Creek MotorSports Inc.), and I was so *proud* of the job, and the things that I learned, but, I also learned to let "the pride-thing" go just so far; or else it dictated my actions. I don't want to be any one's slave. Period! The first year there, I was put into the office in an upper room, with three very senior ladies, and typed forms all day. That's the part that hurt, just because I'm a lefty, I learned how to type so well, and guess what, "into the office." Spending all summer up there was absolutely NO FUN, but hey, I was getting paid (ya $2.10 per hour). Even though we didn't even have air-conditioning.

The second year I said I wouldn't work in the office anymore. They put me out with the other grounds workers. It was so much nicer being outside in the beautiful summertime. But what I really liked was learning all of the horticultural things the experts were so willing to share. Like "be the last person" in your neighborhood to cut your grass in the spring. Your neighbors might give you funny looks, but your grass will luv "ya" That way you are letting the grasses roots go deeper, so when things get dry, they'll stay greener longer. Another tip they gave me, was to NEVER cut your grass in the bright sun light. It is hard on the grass.

Maybe that's what you need, maybe you are co-dependent, or weak in you own self value. But take strength in the fact that somebody (up there↑) knows you, and wants to support you. I didn't say "just to make you happy," He's NOT a vending machine, or a "wish genie". But He wants you to get through this life, with peace in your heart. (third person-spirit).

The point behind all of this, is that legally in Wisconsin, you don't need to wear a helmet. But if you think you can do without "what's from the neck up" and go onto those channels of craziness without one on your head. You are just begging for trouble. Sooner or later your "luck" (which I don't believe in) will <u>Run Out</u>. Bye, All Done, So long, Too Bad, Game over; he' toast, lights-out; their history" now. (all "tavern-talk") that helps No One! Sure they (helmets) can be hot, sure they're not "cool" to wear, as a certain kind of biker. But haven't a lot of us grown up to the point of seeing that good fortune-sooner or later will pass. Then, we'll come to see you in the hospital or else the morgue. "Oh Don't talk like that." I get scolded. Sure it isn't a pretty thought, but hey, the results of a crash aren't pretty either.

Obviously, you now know that I have been DEAD once already, (been there-done that. Did that). Most people will accept things as truth from another who has already done or experienced something, or been somewhere already. <u>Will You?</u>

Here's where it will count. There will be a time when you are going to hear those words, "Depart from me; for I know You NOT!" That's what's in store for the person, who WON'T humble themselves {just enough} to say "You are Right God, I am Wrong-Please Save Me." (Putting a smile on God's face is a real Good Thing

Philippians 2: 14 *"For it is God which worketh in you both to will and to do of his good pleasure."*

I know that you are "going to do, whatever You're going to do" (brilliant statement-huh?). All I ask is, to take these pages you've read and remember, how you're going to "outdo" fate. Playing the "odds" on the roads is like going to Vegas or Atlantic City and thinking you are really going to win, this time, every time.

So, tell me? Is the person sitting there, on the other side of these printed pages, believing themselves to be "too good" to simply (here it comes—humble themselves) to GOD; and say "Your Right God; I'm Wrong, I am a Sinner, and I ask YOU to Save Me . . .: Please" "I AM A SINNER and I can't get to Heaven on my own. I know that the Blood of Jesus, is The Only Thing That Will Get Me There!**"**

I "Believe! I'm not only talking to bikers, but also to their family, friends, companions, kids. I am speaking to everyone who still has a breath to take. I know that you won't believe this, but I really **don't** "despise" Hardley's; it's just that I now have "lived & died on Kawasaki's. See. Even if we're both from Milwaukee.

Here is a question, I ask you to simply ponder. Why would an atheistic person, ever remember or celebrate Memorial Days, or go to a funeral. If the **Dead** *are* **Gone?** What is the point of honoring them? (the dead) If it isn't just "self-serving." Maybe they even have some doubts. Atheistic believers don't need any holidays, they don't believe in "remembrance. After ones "passing" there is NO more need of commemorating or celebrating the past; now is there?

An atheistic person is sure being hypocritical if they "claim" any memory for those that have passed. All you can go is feel sorry for them, and some of us will even pray, for them. "Poor souls."

Chap. 18

Conclusion

Y ou have set and read this book, and maybe you've said to yourself, "who does this guy think he is? Telling me how to live my life and plan for my death. Just like the beginning of the book, he is pretty gutsy.

I don't blame you one bit, for thinking that, of me. If it wasn't for the experiences that I've just shared on these pages, I will sit in heaven one day, with eternal sorrow that I didn't at least try to stop everybody in my hearing (reading) range from just going "over the cliff," to their own destruction. So if you want to get really mad at me, go ahead. I used to analyze all the people who got caught up in the Hardley "craze" (especially around things like the 100th birthday) as being about as individual as *lemmings* running off that Cliff too????? Just be Yourself. Don't put your "faith" in what other people think.

Hey, But if that is **all you want** out of life; I WISH YOU the BEST. And to really get you "goat"

GOD BLES You!

And thanks for putting up with me in this read.
I hope it gave you some chuckles, too.

Now to leave you with the words of a great Orator . . . My Dad

I promised him that someday this would be inscribed on his

Tomb-stone.

Some of the very first words he said to me
(at least the ones I remember are:

"I can't remember the LAST Time I Forgot Anything!"

Please . . . Just remember, Your <u>last breath</u> could really be . . . Hell!

Questions or comments: doa_who_made_it@hotmail.com

doawhomadeit.com

Appendix

A question: Do I need my appendix removed? (sorry)

Many people, have urged me to write this book; now, for

Decades.

I'm not writing it, out of reservation, just apprehension that it is

taken seriously and understood, that nothing that I
have written has been "made up" or embellished.

Please take to heart the things that I have brought to light;
and I pray, that you would "absorb" them into your heart,
to really be honest with yourself, so on
the day that you confront God.

You are found to be one of the "accepted"

Thanks again for your interest.

And I thought that you might find it interesting. I sure did, because I have very little knowledge, or understanding of musical compositions. But I also was "provided with the melody, which I have been told is "so unique". Here are the words, you might find very helpful.

1. Come to me, my lovely daughter, come to me, my handsome boy. My love for you is like no other, my love for you shows through my joy.

   Chorus: 1. For you! For you! I gave it all, For you, For you. Did heed the call, For you For you, I paid the price, I bore the cross, gave all for loss, what 'ere the cost for you.

2. To have you run to me in sadness, To have you run to me in fear, "To have you run to me in gladness, Makes what I did all so clear.

   Chorus: 1. For you! For you! I gave it all, For you, For you, Did heed the call, For You, For You I paid the price I bore the cross, gave all for loss, what 'ere the cost for you.

3. Now you've grown so bold and daring. Now you've gone so far away, now your thought of me are sparing but that's alright, I'm here to stay.

   Chorus:1 For you! For you! I gave it all, For you, For you. Did heed the call, For you, For you, I paid the price, I bore the cross, gave all for loss, what 'ere the cost for you.

4. No matter where you find yourself now, No matter if it's spring or fall, No matter if you don't heed me now, I'm at your side in case you fall